# KISSING STRANGERS
## (THE DAY WE WON THE CUP)

## COMPILED AND EDITED BY GWEN McILROY

ISBN: 0 902804 00 6

The royalties from the sale of this book are being donated for the care and comfort of patients in the Leukaemia Ward of Ninewells Hospital in Dundee.  Thank you for buying it.

Printed and Published by
David Winter and Son Limited
16 Dunsinane Avenue, Dunsinane Industrial Estate
Dundee DD2 3QT Scotland

THIS BOOK IS DEDICATED TO JIM McLEAN, IVAN GOLAC AND ALL THE PLAYERS AND STAFF, PAST AND PRESENT, AT DUNDEE UNITED FOOTBALL CLUB

# Acknowledgements

When you set out to produce a book of this nature you incur many debts along the way. Mine are legion. I was lucky enough to find sources of help and advice at every juncture, so much so that to list them all here would be an impossibility. However there are those to whom I must register an overwhelming vote of thanks, without them this book would never have seen the light of day.

Most of all I have to thank the manager and players for giving us a day that made this possible. Thank you also to each player who spent time talking to me about his experiences of playing in a Cup final and who, consequently, has helped to recapture all those happy memories. I am also especially grateful to Paddy Connolly, Scott Crabbe and Billy McKinlay for allowing me to interview them about an occasion which, for them, was undoubtedly one of mixed emotions.

Needless to say, to each and every contributor I also extend my thanks. Greater love hath no fans than these. Despite their busy lives, each put pen to paper to produce a very personal account which, hopefully, allows the reader to identify with the emotions of the Cup final, and to relive the day through the eyes of those who were there, and some who weren't! Thanks, too, to Dougie Hope, for his contribution.

There were some of the above who went beyond the call of duty. I think especially of Helen Bowman for whom nothing was too much trouble, and Peter Rundo – a man who knows his onions – who supplied me with a great deal of statistical information, much of which I unashamedly plagiarised in the introduction!

I am also indebted to the staff of David Winter and Son for all their assistance, hard work and support, particularly Elma Gibson, Grant Thomson and Jill Stewart.

There are others, too, who I must thank. My husband, Paul, and daughter, Juliet, whose combined knowledge of football and patient good-nature helped me through. To Pauline Miller Judd, Martin Mooney and Abigail Rennie who helped with the proof reading, who never minded when I asked them to look up some obscure piece of information and never once looked at me as if I was someone of diminished responsibility.

I also appreciate the help I received from Henry Smith and Bill Brady of The Scotsman, Kevin McCarra and Graham Spiers of Scotland on Sunday, the staff in the photo departments of The Sun, The Daily Record and The Courier and Evening Telegraph in Dundee. All photographs which appear in this book have been reproduced by kind permission of all the above newspapers.

Special mentions must also go to Mike Clark, Jan Aimer, Mrs Chris Wilson and Sheena and Paul Bailey. Also to Andy McLaren's Mum who put up with umpteen phonecalls from me without so much as a sigh!

And lastly, a special vote of thanks to Dave McPherson and Ally Maxwell!

# CONTENTS

# Introduction

Beneath a sunny sky on 21st May 1994, before a crowd of 38,000 at Hampden Park, Dundee United beat Glasgow Rangers 1 - 0 in the final of the Scottish Cup competition. Many were pleased, many were disappointed. These are the simple facts of the occasion. There is, of course, much more to it than that and if, in years to come, there are those who are inclined to say, "So what?" the hope is that this book, and the very personal accounts contained within it, will go some of the way towards explaining just what this victory meant to those of us who were lucky enough to have been there on the day. And if, along the way, we somehow manage to recapture the atmosphere and the emotion of it all, that too is our intention.

Yes, we did it, Dundee United and their fans on that magical, memorable afternoon. We had long talked of just such a day and if, occasionally, we have to pinch ourselves just to make sure that it wasn't all a dream, there can be few amongst us who aren't convinced that life can offer few things to compare with that day.

If, in the first instance, this book is all about pride and passion, the significance of this victory can only be fully understood by looking at the tale in its entirety. The difficult task is how to be truthful and not exaggerate; in these next few pages I will endeavour to do just that.

## HISTORY IN THE MAKING

If John F Kennedy was correct in his assumption that history has made life difficult for us all, then he'd entirely agree that the burden of history that accompanies the Scottish Cup has indeed made life difficult for United. It isn't, you see, just any old domestic trophy. It's the oldest.

First contested in 1874 by Queens Park and Clydesdale, it became the much-coveted prize at the end of every season (give or take a season or two when war stopped play). The names of the clubs which have been inscribed upon it are many and varied. Inevitably the Old Firm feature prominently (Rangers have won it 26 times, Celtic 29). All the major clubs are there alongside a plethora of sides now regarded as somewhat lowly (amongst them Airdrie, Dumbarton, East Fife and Clyde). There, too, are the now-defunct teams of

Renton, Vale of Leven, St Bernards and Third Lanark. To the chagrin and dismay of most United fans even Dundee FC have won it, never mind the commandment about not coveting thy neighbour's trophy, it has always rankled with United that they have not been able to match, or even outdo, Dundee where this competition was concerned. But, until now, no silversmith has ever been commissioned to take up his tools and engrave the letters which spell out Dundee United on the Scottish Cup.

The road to Hampden for the Tannadice faithful is a well-trodden one, if at first you don't succeed could easily have been United's motto. Having won two League Cups and the Premier Division championship the quest for the Scottish Cup was becoming something of a Holy Grail for United. Incredibly, six Cup final appearances between 1974 and 1991 saw United leave the National Stadium empty-handed and their fans distraught in defeat.

Until the arrival of Jim McLean in 1971, success in this competition was limited to a couple of semi-final appearances under Jerry Kerr, plus the odd notable giant-killing act in the darker Second Division days.

Indeed, when the embryonic Dundee Hibs took their first faltering steps in the League in 1910, entry to the Scottish Cup was by means of the Qualifying Cup. And in the first season Tannadice interest in the Scottish Cup was over by the first Saturday in September. In fact Dundee Hibs had been in existence for four years before they even played their first match in the competition proper and, ironically, in view of later agonies, Queens Park at Hampden were their first opponents. You won't be surprised to learn that the Hampden amateurs won 4 - 2.

Almost exactly half a century would elapse before the club were to register a Scottish Cup victory at Hampden. Eleven more years would pass before United would win at Hampden in a competition, and two further decades would pass before that would occur in the Cup final.

By 1922, things had reached a low ebb as Dundee Hibs crashed out of the Scottish Cup to Broxburn United at Tannadice in the first round, but unlikely as it may seem, things got even worse the following season. League status had been lost as United were the first victims of automatic relegation. Only Celtic's withdrawal from the Scottish Alliance and the offer of their place to Dundee Hibs saved the club from almost complete oblivion. Even then, events on the park were less than auspicious with Dundee Hibs losing 7 - 0 to Airdrie Reserves and 6 - 1 to Dundee's second string! Compounding that was a first round dismissal from the Scottish Cup at the hands of Nithsdale Wanderers who beat the luckless Tannadice men 1 - 0 on Tayside. There were few lower points in the club's history than the season 1922 - 23.

The following season the adoption of the name Dundee United and the installation of Jimmy Brownlie as manager saw United start to blossom.

They were soon to sample First Division football when they pieced together a successful promotion campaign and they managed their best pre-war Cup run during this era. In fact, advancement to the quarter-finals in 1928 - 29 wasn't to be bettered until 1963. It brought United into Cup conflict with Rangers for the first time, although they were beaten 3 - 1 at Ibrox. (It would be another 65 years before United would taste any kind of Cup success against the men from Govan.)

Three years later United exacted full revenge for the embarrassment of the defeat by Nithsdale Wanderers, they dispatched them from the Cup by scoring 14 goals without reply. To this day it remains United's biggest ever victory!

Thereafter only the odd giant-killing act brightened the Tannadice Cup campaigns over the next three decades, most notable was the defeat of Hearts in 1938. But true to form after this victory they promptly slumped to a 5 - 0 defeat at the hands of East Fife, though East Fife were to go on and become the eventual winners of the trophy.

The outbreak of the Second World War precipitated the first Hampden final appearance by Dundee United. Team selections were a problem given the circumstances, but United put together a side which was largely made up of former players who had returned to the area, and they managed to reach the final, even overcoming Airdrie, who had fielded Stanley Matthews as a guest in the semi-final. The scenario which unfolded in the final against Rangers was one which was to become an all-too-familiar one to Tannadice fans. United played well, had a goal chalked off and lost! But, of course, the 1940 Emergency War Cup final does not count in the official records. But the defeat of Celtic, nine years later, certainly did.

The visit of Celtic to Dundee in January 1949, surprisingly their last appearance in the Cup at Tannadice, ended in an astonishing 4 - 3 scoreline in United's favour. It sent shock waves through Scottish football. United may have been a better-than-average Second Division side, and Celtic did only escape relegation by the skin of their teeth the previous season, but even those credentials didn't prepare Scottish football for the shock that was in store. The match is now a part of Tannadice folklore. Quite apart from scoring four times, United had three goals chalked off! This match, more than any other, earned United the nickname, the Terrors. Typically, the Tannadice heroes meekly exited from the competition in the next round against Dumbarton.

Cup exploits over the next decade or so, apart from holding Aberdeen to a draw in 1952 in front of a record domestic crowd at Tannadice, were again ignominious. And in 1953 the players found that, as a consequence of losing 3 - 2 to Berwick in a Cup replay at Tannadice, they were all put on the transfer list.

There was nothing remarkable about the League campaign in the season 1958 - 59 other than the fact that United finished 35th out of Scotland's 37 clubs! The Cup, however, brought what must have been a record as the team was to play four ties in the space of six days. Having played East Stirling in a postponed game on a Monday night which they drew, they were required to replay the following night, again they drew and, after extra time, both teams were to meet again on the Wednesday night. United won this time, 4 - 0, and earned themselves the right to play Third Lanark, three days later. No wonder part-time, and leg-weary, United were beaten 4 - 0 themselves by the men from Cathkin Park.

By 1963 Jerry Kerr had established the club as a fully-fledged member of the First Division and, after the cruelly long winter, United appeared out of their enforced hibernation to reach the penultimate round of the competition for the very first time. Their opponents were Rangers who took an early two goal lead, but the plucky Tannadice side pulled back the deficit. However they were again to fall two goals behind before the half-time interval with Rangers eventually winning the tie 5 - 2, before going on to beat Celtic 3 - 0 in the replayed final.

Four years later Jerry Kerr's men met with some success again in the Cup. They cleared the hurdles of Hearts, Falkirk and Dunfermline to again reach the last four without conceding a goal to an opponent along the way. That record was still intact after losing to Aberdeen in front of 41,000 packed into Dens Park for the semi-final, because it was a tragic own goal which cruelly denied United their first-ever place in a final.

Jim McLean's arrival at Tannadice eventually broke United's duck. It was 1974 and he was in his third full season as manager when his team made it to the semi-final where, having beaten Hearts in a replay, they claimed their first-ever place in the final against Celtic. The game was always going to be something of a mis-match. Celtic had just completed their record-breaking ninth successive League title and had won the Cup more often than any other side. Celtic won the game 3 - 0 but United gave a good account of themselves, especially in the early stages and it was definitely a case of being beaten, but not disgraced.

In 1981 United were to face the other half of the Old Firm, but this time they were the unexpected favourites to win it. Jim McLean had, by then, led the team to win the League Cup - their first-ever trophy, and the Ibrox side had been exhibiting poor League form all season. A last minute penalty awarded to Rangers looked all set to see them collect the trophy after ninety minutes.

But Hamish McAlpine blocked Ian Redford's kick, the game went to extra time and then to a replay where goals in the first twenty minutes by Derek Johnstone and Davie Cooper, both missing from the side for the first tie, virtually killed off United's challenge and although Davie Dodds prodded them back into contention with the club's first goal in a final, Rangers were to come up with another before the break the United fans knew it wasn't going to be their day and, sure enough, Rangers scored again to take the Cup back to Ibrox.

Having won the Premier title in 1983, the Scottish Cup remained the only domestic trophy to elude the United side and hopes of ending that came when United booked another place in a final in 1985 after disposing of Aberdeen in a midweek replay at Tynecastle. Celtic lay in wait for them in the final and for both clubs it was their only hope of a trophy that season. A nervous first-half saw United take the lead thanks to a Stuart Beedie goal. They held on until thirteen minutes before the end of play. A Davie Provan free-kick provided Celtic's first goal and was followed by a Frank McGarvey strike and once more reduced United's Cup hopefuls to tears. The anguish and the grief was all too apparent when the United players sank to the ground as the final whistle blew - little did they know that they would have to live through the same agonies three years later.

In between, in 1987, United were to face St Mirren. It was a momentous season for the club and although the Scottish Cup run took up much of their energy it was also the year of their historic success in the UEFA Cup. Playing Forfar in the Scottish Cup was sandwiched between two European ties against Barcelona. That they beat the Angus club was no small feat given the enormity of the other task in hand. They then went on to face Dundee beating them 3 - 2 at Tynecastle. St Mirren would surely be a pushover. Famous last words. An Ian Ferguson goal, and a poor performance by United, saw them again leave Hampden disconsolate and empty-handed. Days later they also lost the UEFA Cup final.

1988 and it was time for another defeat from Celtic. Two replays against Aberdeen in the semi-final saw them go through to face the Parkhead side. When Kevin Gallagher scored just after half-time it looked as though this time United could hold onto their lead, but an equaliser by Mark McGhee followed by a winning strike from Frank McAvennie with two minutes to go, was once more a kick in the solar plexus for United and their fans.

In the season 1988 - 89 United made it to the quarter-finals to be beaten again by Rangers, while Aberdeen were to be their conquerors in the semi-final in 1990.

1991 saw them once again appear in the final. Having beaten East Fife, Airdrie, Dundee and St Johnstone along the way no-one expected them to lose against Motherwell. A moving occasion with the brothers McLean facing one another only a week after their father had died. It was a gripping final which went to extra-time having been tied at 3 - 3 at the end of the ninety minutes, but Steve Kirk of Motherwell was to score the only goal of the last half-hour and United exited again, in a state of shock and despair, once again they had lost the trophy.

In 1992 and 1993 they never progressed beyond the fourth round going out to Celtic and Aberdeen respectively.

There can be no doubt that the weight of history and experience have dogged United and their fans where the Scottish Cup is concerned. But come the end of January 1994, they set out once more on their quest for treasure. We may never know if they were fuelled by desperation or by hope, and there were many of us who stood on the terracing at Gayfield in Arbroath with heavy hearts. United were having a pretty poor season and few could have believed on that cold, wet afternoon that this was the year that their team would surprise everyone, including I suspect, themselves, by not only reaching their seventh final but also making off with the trophy.

To say they scraped a win at Arbroath is to do United an injustice. There were moments when indeed it looked like it was going to be touch and go but in the main United were in command and goals from Billy McKinlay, Craig Brewster and Scott Crabbe gave them the edge over their 'feisty' opponents even though they managed to score twice in reply.

Then came Motherwell - twice. Two fabulous goals from Craig Brewster, on 19th February should have allowed United to progress having taken a 2 - 1 lead, but in the dying minutes of the game Motherwell drew level and we all trudged off to Fir Park on 1st March and were to be rewarded with a Brian Welsh goal which won the match. Sadly Scott Crabbe broke his leg in this round thus ending his aspirations for Cup glory.

And so on March 12th we found ourselves at Airdie and, when neither team scored, the replay was staged at Tannadice three days later where Billy McKinlay and Andy McLaren both found the net. The two goals were without reply.

When we learned that we were to meet Aberdeen at Hampden we worried that the stadium would again prove to be United's graveyard and, indeed, it seemed it would be so when with only seven minutes on the clock Aberdeen's Duncan Shearer put his side ahead with a goal which owed more to an uncharacteristic blunder by Guido Van de Kamp than to any innate skill on Shearer's part. Constant bombardment of the Aberdeen goal for the rest of the game looked as though it was going to be of no avail when Brian Welsh suddenly appeared in the box, with two minutes to go, and nodded the ball into goal. And the fans went wild. Yet another replay.

Three days later we again arrived at Hampden and, in the seventieth minute of an extremely tense match, Dave Bowman found himself on the end of a Craig Brewster cross. Theo Snelders could only parry the ball into the path of Jim McInally who took several seconds before trundling it into the net. He who hesitates had won the match and after decades of suffering, years of woe and this recent hard-fought campaign, United were into the final. Most agreed that the victory against Aberdeen, on the very soil that had been so hostile, could only augur well for United's chances of finally making off with that most coveted of prizes.

## IVAN GOLAC'S MAGIC

Ivan Golac arrived at Tannadice in the summer of 1993 and the Jim McLean era was over. An era which had seen United climb to unprecedented dizzy heights. McLean's genius and his hard, uncompromising style of management was the driving force behind United's success. There was no mountain they couldn't climb, nothing to which they couldn't aspire. And yet, somehow the Scottish Cup eluded him. A fact which undoubtedly cost McLean more than a few sleepless nights. To lose this trophy once is understandable, two, maybe, three times is hardly cause for concern, but six times is downright carelessness - and no-one knew it more than McLean. If points had been awarded for a record number of losing appearances in the final United would have won hands down. How sad that McLean never sipped champagne from the Scottish Cup (even if, as a teetotaller, he might not have liked its taste).

And how ironical then that the man, who couldn't be more different from Jim McLean if he tried, should saunter into Tannadice and, in his very first year of office, at his very first attempt, win the one prize that had haunted his predecessor. To what can we attribute Golac's success?

Most would put it down to beginner's luck. But surely that can't be the whole story. Golac's style of management must have been a major factor in this victory and certainly the players all seem to say that this was the case. Golac oozes self-confidence and bonhomie, a showman who clearly enjoys the limelight. If some United fans are wary of him because of the poor run of League results that we have witnessed, there are others who worship his anarchic ways. Forget the fact that when he talks he sounds like Chico Marx, Ivan's words in any interview are as pearls of wisdom cast before swine. And his attempts to commune with nature as a training regime are certainly novel. For the Cup final Golac imbued his players with the feeling that they were giants, that the Cup was theirs by right and that they had nothing to fear from Rangers. For players who had heard their previous manager say on occasions that they were unlikely to win this game or that one, Golac's words came close to making them think they were invincible. Jim McLean may have been brutally honest and often he was a realist but Ivan Golac, the dreamer, can clearly motivate his men. He's something of a magician. On this occasion Ivan Golac's magic worked.

## TWELVE GOOD MEN AND TRUE

The foundation of United's success over the years has been the never-ending succession of home-grown talent that has found its way into the first team. United have long been admired for the plethora of players they field who learnt their trade at Tannadice. Rangers, however, have only recently begun to explore this method of team-building, preferring instead to reach for the cheque book rather than turn some spotty-faced youth into a Mark Hateley or an Andy Goram. And let's not forget that much is made of the United connection at Rangers, with manager, Walter Smith and his assistant, Archie Knox, both having served part of their apprenticeships under Jim McLean. Likewise backroom boys, Davie Dodds and Billy Kirkwood wiled away some of their best years at Tannadice. And on the park who can forget that Richard Gough and the £4 million striker, Duncan Ferguson, both spent their formative years at the Tayside club? In some of these cases the link is now tenuous - there's been a lot of water under the Tay Bridge since, say, Smith and Knox last graced the turf at Tannadice, but it all looks good on paper.

Better United teams than this one have turned up in a Hampden final and lost, but there is no denying that the combination of players who made up the United squad was a winning one, and exactly right for the task. This team owed as much to the hand of Jim McLean as to that of Ivan Golac. Men who had been influenced by McLean made up the bulk of the side, but signings such as Craig Brewster, Jerren Nixon and Gordan Petric displayed the Golac touch. There were those in the side who had been involved in other Scottish Cup campaigns and many who had never known what it was like to lose, consequently some were driven by the fear of failing and others were motivated by the will to win. The vigour of youth blended well with the wisdom of experience. There were men of ice and men of fire, there was pride and passion and belief. How could Rangers possibly match such a heady concoction?

## WE ARAB PEOPLE

Call us 'The Tannadice Terrors', or call us 'The Arabs' - either way, they're pretty duff nicknames. Somehow neither has quite the same ring to it as 'The Huns' but there are sections of the United support who are proud to be called Arabs - a name which somewhat unimaginatively seems to have been dreamt up at a time when the Tannadice pitch was more sand than grass. Nowadays at most games you'll see the occasional bewildered soul wandering about Tannadice with a tea-towel on his head, but on the really big occasions the masses don the full regalia. Cup final day was no exception. You were certainly under-dressed if you turned up in a T-shirt and jeans, even with a United scarf round your neck. Your canonicals simply had to be those worn by all the best Bedouins. Failing that, a bright orange curly wig sufficed.

There were 12,000 of us, 19,000 of them and 7,000 assorted others. Being in the minority is not necessarily a handicap on these occasions, it simply means you have to stand up and be counted and no United fan who was there should ever underestimate his or her contribution to the outcome of the game, every one of us as crucial to the team as Craig Brewster or Maurice Malpas. Confidence was at such a high level that it was almost tangible, it stretched down to the pitch and engulfed the players.

United had other allies. Tactical supporters who became armchair Arabs for the day. These included, the anti-Rangers faction which included, I suspect, the fans of almost every other club in Scotland. Probably only those who supported Rangers and Dundee were less than pleased by the result. There was even the lobby who might simply have been fed up with United forever whingeing and moaning about their lack of success at Hampden who wanted United to win merely to shut them up. I have to say that I even met a few Rangers fans who, after the match, announced that they didn't actually mind that United had won. Patronising gits!

Spare a thought, however, for the poor soul who, having been caught up in a bit of a fracas before the match, found himself frog-marched off to the nearest Police station. And there he spent the night. On being released the following morning, he was wandering round Glasgow still wearing his United strip looking so forlorn that when he encountered some Rangers supporters they asked him why he looked so down in the dumps. They sympathised when they heard his tale of woe, but pointed out that surely the result would have been some compensation for his loss of liberty. He was, in fact, quite surprised to learn that United had won. The Police had told him that the result had been 3 - 1 to Rangers! He immediately set off, in high spirits, to join the party in Dundee.


## HAMPDEN REVISITED

No matter how vigorously they deny it, most United fans find Hampden a hostile place, the home of the hoodoo and amateur side, Queens Park. Before refurbishment some say it was a national disgrace, others it was the grand old lady of Mount Florida. Set amongst some of the finest of Glasgow's tenements it has presided over the area since 1903. There have been rebuilding schemes throughout that time, and even plans to demolish the National Stadium altogether. In the wake of the Hillsborough disaster, and in response to the Taylor Report, clubs throughout the land were having to upgrade their stadia and the time had come to decide whether or not the future of Hampden lay with the builders or the demolition squads. At a cost of £24 million the ground is now in the hands of the construction companies and only the South Stand, and the toilets, have yet to be upgraded. It all looks quite wonderful, especially just after you've watched your team win the Scottish Cup there, a stately place which is not pompous or architecturally outrageous.

And the transformation was just what we needed. This was Hampden and, then again, it wasn't. A place that held no fears, none whatsoever.

## THE MAN IN THE MIDDLE

A few words about the referee - and we won't even mention the disputed penalty! This was Dougie Hope's last official engagement. He'd been running up and down football pitches for nigh on twenty-six years and it was time to hang up his whistle. In real life he's a Reporter to the Children's Panel and is greatly respected both on and off the field. It must have been an emotional day for him, he could have gone out in a blaze of controversy by waving cards and blowing his whistle like there was no tomorrow. Instead he was almost inconspicuous, the hallmark of a good referee, and can regard his contribution to the whole affair as an important one.

## THE BEAUTIFUL GAME

If much of what follows in this book is about the emotion of the day this, perhaps, is the place to take a dispassionate look at the match - minute by minute - and I am indebted to Pete Rundo who supplied the following report.

Saturday 21st May 1994

TENNANTS SCOTTISH CUP FINAL

United 1        Rangers 0
*Brewster*

UNITED:    Van de Kamp, Cleland, Malpas, McInally, Petric, Welsh, Bowman, McKinlay, McLaren (Nixon 83), Brewster, Dailly. Substitute not used: Bollan.

RANGERS:  Maxwell, Stevens (Mikhailitchenko 24), Robertson, Gough, McPherson, McCall, Murray, I Ferguson, McCoist (D Ferguson 73), Hateley, Durie.

REFEREE:  D D Hope (Erskine)

CROWD:    38,000

**3.00pm**   United kicked off.

**3.01**  Just under a minute on the clock and we had the first foul of the match when Hateley bundled Malpas to the ground as they went up for a high ball.

**3.05**  Petric was brought down 30 yards outside the box, but Brewster's free kick from that distance was blocked.

**3.07**  Malpas was forced to concede the first corner of the game as he knocked a Gary Stevens cross to safety.

**3.08**  Rangers had their first attempt on goal as Gordon Durie made ground on the left before escaping from Dave Bowman, his shot sailed over.

**3.09**  Rangers won a second corner. McPherson's header from Durie's cross was on target but McInally was there to block it on the line.

**3.11**  The first moment of controversy in the match. United broke to the other end, quickly turning defence into attack. Craig Brewster's beautiful reverse pass sent Alex Cleland racing clear into the box, but he was impeded from behind by Ian Ferguson and went tumbling over Maxwell. Despite strong appeals by the United players no penalty was forthcoming.

**3.13**  Ally McCoist was brought down by Gordan Petric just inside his own area and, from a dangerous position, Hateley curled the ball inches wide of the angle of bar and post.

**3.17**  Craig Brewster was on the end of a Christian Dailly cross but got under the ball to send his header well over the bar.

**3.20**  Christian Dailly sprung the Ibrox side's offside trap, but Maxwell got down to cut out his cross just before it reached Brewster.

**3.21**  The first real stoppage of the game as play was held up to allow Gary Stevens to receive treatment. As soon as play resumed Andy McLaren crossed from a Brewster assist and Dailly headed the ball narrowly past the near post.

**3.25**  Stevens was no longer able to carry on after picking up an injury and Alexei Mikhailitchenko came on to replace him.

**3.27**  Maurice Malpas rescued a tricky situation when the ball was played through to McCoist.

**3.28**  Hateley intelligently ran onto a McCall through ball but fired just wide.

**3.31**  Full-back David Robertson strode forward to join the attack, but blasted the ball over the bar.

3.33   Play was held up as Maurice Malpas received treatment.

3.34   Jim McInally blocked a Dave McPherson shot.

3.38   Craig Brewster had a shooting opportunity but his effort lacked composure.

3.42   Craig Brewster again had a shooting opportunity when he unleashed a 20-yarder which had Maxwell at full stretch to tip past the post.

3.47   The half-time whistle went.

3.57   Rangers kicked off the second-half.

3.59   United took the lead. McPherson tried to usher the ball back to Maxwell, but was forced to pass it back from close range. Dailly, who had been harrying him then charged down Maxwell's clearance and controlled the ball before rolling a shot towards goal, the ball hit the inside of the far post and bounced off it into the path of Brewster who thumped it into the net.

4.03   Gough conceded a corner and from it McInally shot high and wide.

4.04   Maxwell was forced to push an Andy McLaren corner round the post.

4.07   Mikhailitchenko sent in a fearsome shot which Guido Van de Kamp tipped over the bar.

4.10   A Mikhailitchenko shot hit the side netting.

4.12   Malpas was booked for body-checking a Hateley run.

4.13   Brian Welsh cleared a dangerous looking corner.

4.15   More pressure from Rangers, this time from McCall, but Gordon Petric stole the ball from him but conceded a corner. Van de Kamp came to the rescue as the ball came in from the cornerflag.

4.18   McCoist tried a weak shot which was easily saved by Van de Kamp.

4.20   McPherson tried a long shot to no avail.

4.21   United broke out of defence and Maxwell had to save from McInally.

4.22   Mikhailitchenko blasted a shot which winded Malpas as he blocked it.

4.23   Panic in the United defence when a volley from Hateley slipped out of Van de Kamp's hands, he quickly retrieved it.

4.25   Ally McCoist was replaced by Duncan Ferguson

4.27   McPherson tried another shot from 20 yards out but it was saved.

4.29   Neil Murray sent in a cross which was eventually scrambled to safety by the United reabguard.

4.30  Danger as Mikhailitchenko was brought down on the edge of the box, but Ferguson's free kick was blocked.

4.35  Jerren Nixon replaced Andy McLaren.

4.36  Brewster ran onto a McInally pass and raced towards goal, his shot was turned round the post by Maxwell.

4.38  Durie and Nixon were both booked following a foul by Ferguson on the United striker.

4.42  Yet again McPherson tried a shot, this time from the edge of the box, but it failed to penetrate the defence.

4.44  Referee Dougie Hope blew the full-time whistle and at long last United had won the Scottish Cup.

# A DAY FOR KISSING STRANGERS

## *Helen Bowman*

For eleven years Helen Bowman has been David Bowman's partner, companion, confidante and staunch supporter, and the remarkable thing is that marriage, for them, didn't ruin a beautiful friendship! They have two daughters, Jemma and Rebecca. After the despair and disappointment of previous Scottish Cup finals Helen vowed that if Dundee United made it to Hampden this year she would not be there.

---

# HELPLESS

The tyranny which football exerts over the life of the average football supporter is as nothing compared to that which governs the lives of those for whom football is more than just a pastime. Namely the players and their families. Certainly the rewards for those in the top echelons of the game can provide a comfortable, sometimes opulent, lifestyle. But consider. The precariousness inherent in football must ensure that there is never a hint of complacency in the household of any player.

Insecurity is the name of the game. Reliant on bonuses and incentives to supplement his income the ever-present threats of injury and loss of form are the player's constant companions. Moreover, despite the considerable efforts of the Player's Union, the footballer is still almost wholly controlled by his club like some latter-day fief or serf; and because he is always subject to the whim of his manager he can fall from grace in an instant. Many do.

Even if he is lucky, a footballer cannot expect to stay in the game, except in the rarest of cases, beyond thirty-five or thirty-six. The chances of becoming a manager or a coach, once he's discarded his boots, are not high. There are more players than there are clubs. Every season is a season nearer to retirement and the time to find a new way of earning a living when most men in other jobs haven't even reached the peak of their careers. For men who have often known no way of life other than football, the arrival of the thirtieth birthday party must hold more than a few terrors, amongst them the thought that the past is always going to be better than the future. Football can be a cruel master.

As self-evident as these facts may be, who amongst the fans really cares what becomes of a one-time hero once his playing days are behind him? Who indeed? It is only a matter of consequence to the player and his immediate family.

When faced with such a gloomy prospect, Helen Bowman must wonder what on earth possessed her to marry a footballer for, coupled with the slings and arrows of outrageous fortune, there are the iconoclastic boo-boys and the vitriolic scribes of the tabloid press to contend with. And no-one could pretend that such things do not hurt. They do. Other inconveniences must include living with the self-discipline demanded by regular training, and the fact that being married to someone with such a high profile who is as easily recognisable as David Bowman is, must mean that every family outing will be interrupted by the constant attentions of strangers. He has many admirers and probably a few enemies, amongst whom he would probably count one or two Dundee fans.

To be the wife of a footballer must take fortitude, stamina, the skin of an armadillo and a kind of madness to want it. A sense of humour is also an asset. All in all it takes an extraordinary kind of woman. Enter Helen Bowman who is unfalteringly spontaneous, honest and funny. She is also exceedingly beautiful in every sense of the word, has personality and guts, and is as wise as she is intelligent. Above all, she is philosophical in outlook. She regards life as something of an adventure. All things considered Helen Bowman is some lady!

She was only seventeen when she fell head-over-heels for the promising young Hearts midfielder and from then on she has shared his moments of glory and all his misery. And like Edith Piaf she'll tell you that she has no regrets, that the good times far outweigh the bad and, anyway who, in the current economic climate, can say that his or her job is any more secure than that of those who earn their living by playing football? Very few.

Helen Bowman, however, is married to two men. There's David Bowman the footballer whose public image is that of a hard-tackling, no-holds-barred midfielder who learnt his trade in the school of hard knocks and who is known as a man who gives a hundred percent in every game. A favourite with the fans, the scourge of referees and opposition players alike. David Bowman the warrior. David Bowman the winner. Headstrong and quixotic. A man's man for a' that!

But David Bowman the family man is a very different character. Away from the field he is a gentle man. Sensitive, quiet and thoughtful. He hates the thought that anyone might get the impression that he is big-headed and shies away from the limelight as much as possible. In a house peopled by women he is very much at home in women's company and he takes his responsibilities as a husband and father very seriously. A woman's man, in fact.

In many ways Helen Bowman is also married to Dundee United. When David signed for the club in 1986 she fell in love with the city of Dundee and with the club and its fans. You can see her at almost every match at Tannadice - tense and engrossed. It is the family atmosphere at the club that she finds most appealing. She feels involved on a day-to-day basis, and most of the friends she considers to be her closest have been made through her association with United.

Why then, all things considered, did Helen Bowman decide, on the day that her husband was playing one of the most important games of his career, to go shopping? Especially when the rest of us didn't want to miss a moment of the match.

Two reasons.

The first being that she simply could not bear to watch. The memories associated with previous Cup finals were still too fresh and painful. Most especially she is still haunted by the game against Motherwell in 1991. It mattered little that United gave one of their finest performances that day, it mattered even less that it had been an epic game and one which is regarded as a yardstick by which all other finals are judged. It mattered hardly a jot that David was voted Man of the Match that day for all she remembers is how dejected and disappointed he looked as he stood in the foyer at Hampden. And while he and the other players were collecting their runners-up medals Helen was sitting in the car park crying. She admits she's shed many tears in pursuit of this trophy. She could not bear to shed any more, and so logic and inclination dictated that it would be advisable to give this game a miss. She just wasn't sure that United would win. It wasn't that she didn't have faith, she knew that the team could do it - but she just wasn't confident that this was the day that they would. And anyway, she didn't want to ruin the game for those around her.

Mainly, however, it was an overriding, all-consuming sense of being utterly helpless that stopped her going to Hampden. David Bowman wanted to win that Cup with almost every fibre of his being. He is not an acquisitive man by nature but the one thing that meant so much to him was one of the few things beyond Helen's control to give him. The frustration and sense of powerlessness that this engendered further persuaded her to stay away. And because she knew that, despite their closeness, the moment her husband stepped out into the Hampden sunshine she could do nothing to help him and that his concentration would be so complete, it would make no difference whatsoever whether she was there in body or just in spirit.

And, as she relives her day, you are reminded of that classic episode of the 'Likely Lads' in which the twosome spent the best part of their day strenuously avoiding hearing the score of a fictitious international match - England versus Bulgaria. The extraordinary lengths they went to just so that they could watch the match on television that night, without knowing the outcome, provided much mirth and merriment for viewers. In Helen's case she went through hell during the ninety minutes that United faced Rangers but nonetheless resolved not to attempt to find out the score until it was all over - that way she might.. just might.. hold onto her sanity. And come what may she would deal with the emotional fall-out as, and when, it occurred.

And so it was that at midday she set out for Glasgow with two friends. Two friends to whom she will remain eternally grateful for their support and understanding throughout the day. She found herself in Princes Square wandering in and out of the chic designer shops in an aimless, detached fashion. Over lunch she found it hard to swallow the fact that everywhere she looked all she could see was normality. Normal people doing, well, normal things. Inside her she was screaming, 'How can you all be so normal when only a few miles away the Scottish Cup final is about to kick-off?' And quite by chance she met a couple from Dundee and was able relieve some of the tension as she chatted about the game.

A tour of the department stores was next on the agenda, taking great care to avoid the electrical departments in case a glimpse of a television screen would reveal the dreaded scoreline. By half-time, her friends tell her she was so pale she looked ghostly. She felt faint. She was, she says, reduced to scanning the faces of the other shoppers for some kind of clue. This was Glasgow and so it would seem logical to suppose that if the people around her looked happy then Rangers must be winning. But to her dismay she was met with little more than a wall of inscrutability. And all the while she kept wondering how David was coping.

Accidentally the three friends passed the electrical department in Frasers. It seemed remarkably quiet. Was this a hopeful sign or was she clutching at straws? Coffee time and Helen's nerves were beginning to get the better of her - so much so she even considered taking up smoking in an effort to keep calm!

With five minutes of normal time remaining it occurred to her that she must have looked at every conceivable household item under the sun. She'd looked at them, but not really seen them at all. With only four minutes of normal time remaining her friend, who had sneaked away to ascertain the score, informed her that United were winning 1 - 0. 'Omigod!' she thought gazing at some towels, 'But this is Glasgow, and they always add five minutes onto the game if Rangers are losing. Always.'

And so it was that with three minutes of normal time remaining, Helen Bowman and her two friends raced towards the electrical department arriving in front of a television set just as the ball at Hampden was going out of play. Jerren Nixon went to pick it up and the final whistle blew. And there was David Bowman and Jim McInally, exactly eight years on from the day that they both signed for United, standing side by side - grinning from ear to ear.

And what did Mrs Bowman do? She hugged her friends, she hugged the sales assistants. She hugged everyone in sight. She cried a lot too.

And then it was time to make a mad dash to Hampden to hug the one person that she wanted most to hug. As luck would have it, the taxi driver who picked her up turned out to be a Rangers' fan - and none too pleased with the afternoon's events. But by the time he'd arrived at the national stadium he was certainly feeling that victory for Dundee United was no bad thing.

And if you ask her if she feels that by avoiding the game she missed being part of an historic and momentous event, she'll tell you that that was only a small part of the experience. For her the journey home with the team and their wives and girlfriends was an equally memorable experience (more tears!). And she will never forget the colour, the emotion and the wonderful reception given to the team the next day in the city centre. Regrets? She might well echo Frank Sinatra's sentiments, 'a few, but then again too few to mention.' She did it her way!

## *Paul Chima*

Born in India in 1953, Paul Chima moved to Dundee when he was nine months old. He was a pupil at Morgan Academy and then went on to study medicine at Dundee University between 1971 - 1977. He now lives in Edinburgh and is a General Practitioner at Stoneyburn in West Lothian. With the help of his brother, Dal, Paul has written about his day. He believes he knows the secret of United's success.

# SEVENTH HEAVEN

The dawn of yet another Cup final, the seventh of the elusive variety. A day like any other to most inhabitants of our planet, but there exists a special breed on earth, a super sub-species whose resilience and optimism know no bounds and to those, today was another chance, perhaps even the final chance to experience the ultimate footballing high of winning 'the Cup'.

Would this be the occasion? Many had long since given up hope, reluctantly adopting the role of the eternal gallant loser, and to others winning the Scottish Cup was now less important than avoiding the emasculating effect of losing another final. I had been to all seven, from United's first appearance in 1974 with a bunch of fellow medical students forming a knot amongst the sparse United support, when we were just thrilled to be there; to the vastly disappointing defeat by St Mirren with perhaps our finest team; and the gala occasion against Motherwell witnessing perhaps the best final ever played, but departing on every occasion with a weary depressive demeanor, the triumphant echoes of the opposition fans as a distinct mocking epitaph. Was it all that important that the Cup was finally adorned with the name of Dundee United? There were times when a preoccupation with this quest seemed inconsequential and petty, the world had its crises, Eastern Europe, Bosnia, Latin dictatorships, African poverty and yet I suspected strongly that if most United fans were asked for their solitary wish to be granted world peace would came a distant, but laudable, second to winning the Scottish Cup!

A morning such as this conjured up distant memories, some happily reflected upon, some humorous, some tip-toeing stealthily from long subjugated recess of the sub-conscious, memories that could only be truly exorcised by the ultimate victory. Losing our 'lucky' scarf out of the car window on our way to the St Mirren final. After much deliberation, a mad dash across four lanes of speeding traffic and a central reservation retrieved it, only for it to be returned with disgust to same said spot on the journey home from yet another disappointment. Memories of fantastic United supports over the years refusing to allow disappointment to mar occasion, priding themselves on good sportsmanship, bearing all philosophically. Who can ever forget the marvellous Tannadice support cheering opponents and home players alike after the UEFA Cup final defeat? Such genuine magnanimity in defeat is indeed rare in the annals of modern sport and many a proud tear was shed that evening. Other memories reflect the keen anticipation for each competition that resurfaces season after season. The nerve-ridden experience of each match, a heady and stomach-churning concoction of enjoyment, apprehension, belief and disbelief in equal part and the inevitable rationalisation of defeat. Those who see football as only a game clearly do not understand the passions of the ritual, they fail to comprehend the sense of identity engendered and do not see the significance of the united will, the coming together of several thousands of disparate souls which represents the full spectrum of societies' classes making sport and not war.

Having travelled independently to previous finals I resolved early on to change this pattern, and having taken the Edinburgh Supporters' Club bus to every round it was not a difficult decision to do so for the final. I had started travelling with the club some five to six years previously. I left Dundee in 1979 but kept on my season ticket for Tannadice and drove to most games not realising that United's support extended to travellers from other cities. The club is a very well-organized one with a friendly atmosphere which makes travelling with them a pleasure. A wide spectrum of personalities and professions is represented and anyone with an image of soccer rowdies would be very pleasantly surprised.

We set off full of our usual optimism shepherded paternally by Jim Gardiner - our secretary and by his wife, Hazel (the only pessimist aboard). I had arranged to meet my brother, Dal, and some of his friends in Rutherglen where I expected a small gathering of United fans. The scene that met me after I had made my way to the upper level of a typically luxurious west coast hostelry, accompanied by the strains of communal singing, was quite staggering. Several hundred happy souls bedecked in tangerine and black, in various stages of revelry were having a party that was as good-natured as it was exuberant and anarchic. The scene was quite unforgettable and lives with me to this day. It was a perfect example of a large crowd in a very confined space enjoying a wild, raucous, alcohol-fuelled celebration that to the outsider may well have appeared threatening (in fact it provoked a sinister response as you will read later) but never got out of hand or was marred by incidents of unpleasantness. The scene still defies belief, given that it was a pre-match celebration. Complete strangers embracing, kissing, dancing (often on, occasionally under, tables) and making life-long, transient friendships. It was, however, very difficult to dispel the suspicion that the celebrations were being held before the match because the prospect of post-match ones were unlikely. This did not inspire confidence. Any such thoughts, however, seemed churlish, almost treasonable, when one surveyed the exuberant, joyous and apparently carefree faces. If only a fraction of their bravado and sense of invincibility could be carried onto the field of play there would be no question of the outcome. As comforting as it was to remain within the enclave of reassurance and confidence, kick-off rapidly approached and it was time to leave behind the communal self-delusion and embark on the trek to reality.

Entering into the bright sunshine, leaving behind the darkened interior it took some moments for our eyes to adjust. We had left in batches and there were several dozen of us within some yards of the bar entrance. We suddenly became aware of a very large crowd of youths appearing from around a corner a few hundred yards ahead of us and running towards us at speed, shouting and screaming, many dressed in the colours of our opponents and brandishing bottles and other weapons. There was an initial hesitation as our brains struggled to take in this sudden transformation of atmosphere and then, as one, we turned to seek the sanctuary of our recently-deserted refuge. Only one half of the swing doors was unlocked - making our scramble that much more desperate and, as we pushed and shoved against each other - feelings of self preservation to the fore, the sense of panic that appears in such situations became only too apparent. To be suddenly confronted by the reality of violence, to be at the mercy of these young thugs, to be hemmed in by my fellow victims was perhaps the most frightening experience of my life, paralleled only by a very nasty several-hundred-yard fall while skiing two years ago. Ski-tow pylons don't carry knives and don't screech and holler in guttural accents, so this episode had a more immediate intensity. I was trapped against the closed door unable to move in any direction, aware that there were only half a dozen or so people immediately behind me buffering me from the crowd that had now arrived in our midst. As I saw one poor chap, only a couple of feet behind me, pulled out of the huddle to be confronted by a knife and felt a bottle whizzing past me and smash against the door in front, inches from my head, all I could do was pull my jacket over my head for protection and reacquaint myself with prayers to every religion known to man, all thoughts of lifelong agnosticism suddenly dispelled. It would not be over-dramatic to admit that I genuinely feared that some serious hurt was about to be inflicted on my person.

Just as hopes of laps of honour in the sun were being forced aside by the expectation of the antiseptic smell of hospital wards the cavalry arrived in the guise of Strathclyde's finest constabulary. They were not exactly very polite, sympathetic or understanding to many of the United fans who had been forced (with varying degrees of enthusiasm) to defend themselves, but they were a very welcome sight to those of us with more gentle dispositions. Unfortunately just about as many United fans as their attackers were arrested, despite an attempted intervention by us on behalf of those who had simply been caught up in the melee. Requests for a sizable escort for the rest of our journey also fell on deaf ears. Unfortunately it often seems that rational discussion, and our beloved constabulary in action, are mutually incompatible. I later heard that at least two United supporters had been stabbed and hospitalised.

To arrive at Hampden Park in one piece was quite a relief, the waves of nausea and the sense of foreboding evaporated as anticipation replaced the revulsion at some elements of society who see particular events as opportunities for destruction rather than celebration. Kissing strangers is an alien concept to them, assaulting them is much more to their liking. It makes a mockery of certain well-known west coast football clubs whose representatives continually protest that their legions contain no anti-social elements and that, on a few well-publicised occasions, it was in fact foreign police forces that precipitated violence. The distaste of this episode was soon dispelled by the all-singing, all-dancing festival atmosphere created by the United support in the crowd. Those of us there will never forget the fiesta in the sun, as we waited for a match that half of you hoped would never start - for the game brought with it reality. The conclusion of the match could only bring the inevitable all-consuming disappointment and ignominious retreat to Dundee. Genuine hopes of optimism in the more realistic of us had to fade, after all we were playing the great Glasgow Rangers. God's own team, favoured by Freemasons and Orange Orders the world over. Darlings of the Scottish media, favourites always for the Scottish League championship, Scottish Cup, European Cup, World Cup and the Grand National! This team of highly paid professionals, perfect examples of manhood with barely a flaw between them, could not possibly lose to a provincial club of such a lowly stature as Dundee United, albeit that many acknowledged United to be amongst the best and most skillful teams in the land.

The final whistle sounded and joy was unleashed with full force amongst the United legions. The moment had finally arrived, jinxes ended, predictions dumbfounded, long-held dreams realised - the Scottish Cup was at last bedecked with tangerine and black ribbons. The party that had started many hours earlier, and had continued almost unabated through the afternoon, could now explode in its full glory in the knowledge that nothing could curtail it. It was someone else's turn to leave the slopes of Hampden early. There was singing and dancing, fully grown men unashamedly shedding tears, some perhaps still slightly unable to accept the reality of the triumph - possibly fearful that exaltations might awaken them from this land of dreams. Fears of an anti-climax were dispelled as fans, players, manager and back-room staff continued the celebrations long after the final whistle. Edicts by the SFA banning displays of exuberance were ignored, did they ever have any chance of being obeyed if United triumphed? The grins on the faces of the players interviewed, the cavortings of recent-signings - Petric and Nixon, the ecstasy of the goalscorer - Brewster and the extrovert display by Ivan Golac, with the protracted carnival atmosphere generated by the fans as a backdrop, amply demonstrated what a truly unique triumph we were witnessing, and I am certain the majority of Scotland joined in. Jim McLean who had done so much to create the modern-day success that is Dundee United, could afford to stand on the sidelines and fully savour the enormity of his achievement.

Two cameos from Hampden helped to illustrate what winning the Cup has meant to some. One group of fans of our acquaintance could take the strain no longer with almost twenty minutes left to play. They had seen leads squandered before, witnessed equalising and winning goals scored against us more than once, and with United one goal up the prospect of watching Rangers attempting to do the same was too much to bear. They retired to the sanctity of the Hampden toilets for solitude and prayer sending out an emissary at regular occasions for updates on the situation, only to emerge on the final whistle.

Another acquaintance was due to meet some friends from the south at Buchanan Street Bus Station in Glasgow at 12.45pm. The bus he boarded from Dundee broke down five minutes away from the city. Another bus arrived and they were asked to transfer. After a short stop in Perth they headed off and eventually passed over the Forth Road Bridge. At South Queensferry the driver asked if anyone was going to Glasgow, as most were, and informed them that they were on the wrong bus. The driver offered to take them into the bus station in Edinburgh where they arrived at 2.30pm after encountering several traffic jams. Despite a hectic dash to Waverley Station they missed a train by two minutes and the following one deposited them in Glasgow at 4.35pm just in time the watch the last five minutes of the game on television. Of such tales are folklore made.

Now that the dust has settled, the plaudits acknowledged and the rewards savoured the need for analysis is pressing. After so many attempts what tactical ploy had finally won the day? Five at the back? Three up front? One-touch football? New training techniques? NO! The answer was elusive but obvious, simple yet devastating. My brother and I each wore the same pairs of boxer shorts to every round. We had tried many similar ploys in the past, going to the same pre-match restaurant, same pub, wearing the same clothes - jumpers, jackets, trousers etc. Now we had found the answer, forget about sitting back when a goal up and defending like mad, never mind getting the players in peak condition - there's no need for complicated tactics. NO! In future all United fans should follow this lead, wearing the same boxers to each Cup game, washed between each round preferably!

# *Paddy Connolly*

At 24 Paddy Connolly's career at Tannadice spans eight years – man and boy. An industrious striker who is a menace to defences and, whether he's flying down the wing or racing through the centre, he can turn a match with a moment's brilliance. Like most strikers he comes in for some harsh treatment during the course of a game and yet, you'll never see him lose his temper, even under the severest pressure. His smile can light up the whole football pitch …

---

# BEHIND THE SMILE

There can be few more pleasing sights in football - the small guy with the ball who is willing to take on the big guy in the defence and beat him before making for goal. David and Goliath. Paddy Connolly and, well, any defender you care to name. Watch him run at opposition players twice his height and you're seized by strange feelings of protectiveness. After all, he's only 5ft 8in, and in the heightist world of football that's usually described as diminutive, but in the eyes of most United fans Paddy is a giant!

Always a player who caught the eye, it was in the season 1992/93 that he really shone for it was during this period that Connolly and not, as many might think, the £4 million striker - Duncan Ferguson, who was United's top scorer and who was, by general consensus, player of the season. Connolly and Ferguson developed quite an understanding on the park. Theirs proved to be a good marriage which succeeded in creating most of United's chances. Where Ferguson, tall and angular, was a man of pace and fire, Connolly's small, neat figure brought calmness and guile to the attack.

To watch Connolly at his best is a delight. He's a master at allowing the ball to run. He lets it come and then turns with it instead of stopping it, using the element of surprise to get away from his marker. From then on it's his darting pace and sudden changes of direction which enable him to take on other men and beat them. In the season prior to Ivan Golac's accession to the Tannadice helm we watched Connolly grow in stature and confidence. And confidence, the player readily admits, is an important element in his game, but it is a fragile and delicate commodity and can be dented in an instant. And the only thing that can be said with any certainty about lack of confidence is that it comes to every player, and every team, at some juncture.

The arrival of a new manager at any club is usually accompanied by wholesale changes at every level. Paddy is the first to recognise this. In the main, Golac has eased himself into the job and the casualties amongst the playing staff were not as widespread as many anticipated. Given Connolly's striking record it was unlikely that he had much to fear but, as it turned out, his was a season characterised by uncertainly. Despite the fact that his name was to be found on the teamsheet on forty occasions last season he, nonetheless, probably never knew if he was going to be in or out of the team or, if selected, if he would he spend inordinate amounts of the game on the substitutes' bench. Moreover, finding himself transfer-listed every now and again can't have helped his self-confidence. When you don't know what you've done wrong it must be particularly frustrating. Does he complain? Does he rant and rave and rail against the injustice of it all? He does not. Such is his nature that he just grits his teeth in a determined fashion and works hard in the hope that he'll hold onto a place.

You'd think that every player who played in any of the Cup qualifying rounds would feel entitled to lay claim to have played a part in the eventual victory and might be considered worthy of a winner's medal. But it doesn't work like that and few players seem to want it any other way. "Medals belong only to those who take part on the day." Connolly states emphatically.

He made two appearances along the road to Hampden. He played in the first game against Arbroath in January, which United won 3 - 2, and in the home tie against Motherwell in February which ended in a 2 - 2 draw.

What he remembers most about the match at Gayfield was that it was here that he received the first booking of his career, a matter of some concern to someone who is neither ill-tempered nor malicious on the field. "The match was a difficult one and we had to fight hard to win it. The weather conditions were awful - cold, wet and windy and when Arbroath got their two goals in the second-half of the game there were those who were quick to say that United tend to underestimate the so-called smaller sides." Paddy Connolly pooh-poohs this supposition. "Clubs from the lower divisions," he says, "often feel that when they are on home territory the only way to try to get a result is to attack right from the off - and they always make it hard for Premier League sides." United have had enough experience of playing the lower orders (and enough frights) to know that they underestimate them at their peril.

The Motherwell game was a heart-breaker. Two stunning goals from Craig Brewster (one of which owed much to the part played by Connolly) should easily have won the game, despite the fact that Motherwell had taken the lead in the 31st minute, but a very late equaliser by the visitors left the home fans and the United players shell-shocked, with a week to wait for the replay at Fir Park. Paddy was dropped for that game and failed to make a return for any of the subsequent qualifying games.

Prior to the Cup final itself many felt that Connolly had played enough games throughout the season, and had acquitted himself well enough in them, to merit consideration for inclusion in the squad. If Ivan Golac could not find room for him in the starting eleven, surely the number 12 or number 14 jersey was up for grabs. Connolly himself hoped that he might just be in luck, not least because his mother was making the trip over from Donegal for the match, even though Paddy had warned her there was only a slim chance of him playing. It is likely that Mrs Connolly Senior would have paid small attention to his caveat. Ask any player, they'll tell you that to their families they are the most important player in any team, they believe that only injury or suspension keep them out of the side. Only a madman of a manager would compile a teamsheet where their son/brother/husband's name wasn't first on it. Mrs Connolly is no different. Paddy is her blue-eyed boy (except that his eyes are the greenest green you've ever seen!).

And when on the Thursday before the game the happy band of players set off for East Kilbride and Paddy climbed aboard the coach it was a fingers-crossed farewell from all the Connolly clan. The next time they were to meet was in the stand at Hampden. The player himself says, "As I set off I was determined to have a good time. Everyone was relaxed and it just rubbed off on me, even though I did spend much of the time wondering if I would be in the team." And a good time, it seems, was had by all. A plush hotel with all the trimmings and a day out at the races, amongst other delights, all served to soothe nerves. On Friday the starting line-up was announced. No Connolly. No Perry. No Nixon. And no Bollan either. So there was still a fifty-fifty chance that any two from this quartet of hopefuls could be called upon as substitutes.

And when it became clear that Mary Perry and Paddy Connolly were surplus to requirements it must have taken considerable skill to hide their disappointment. They were bound to feel left out and hurt but their immediate reaction was to treat the decision with wry humour rather than succumb to despair. For Paddy it was important not to show what he was feeling inside and then perhaps the pain would go away. And even though it was a bitter personal blow to him, Paddy is neither mean-spirited nor petty -

amazingly he says he felt more disappointment for Billy McKinlay and Scott Crabbe than he did for himself because they had both had to live with the knowledge that they would not take part for much longer than he had.

And yet when you talk to him about his feelings during the match and suggest that any player who is dropped from the team is bound to experience a terrible conflict he agrees. It is difficult not to feel some degree of pleasure when the side gets beaten when you're not playing because in the first instance none of the blame can be attached to you and secondly, you are once more in contention for a place. You are sad, too, for your team-mates and the club. But Paddy was determined that he would savour as much of the day as possible and take pleasure in it for the others. He sat on the bus and in the dressing-room listening to the talk of tactics and the game plan. And then he wished the others all the best and meant it, before he walked away.

And so Paddy Connolly sat in the stand trying to come to terms with his own sense of solitude, trying to watch the game through reasonable eyes. It was easy, he says, to become engrossed in the play and to will the team to win. And when they did his immediate feelings were of sheer joy.

And when the final whistle blows and all the players run to the fans, there's Paddy hugging the others and smiling for the cameras and you'd never know that inside he's devastated, that suddenly it hit him that when you're not involved it means nothing to you on a personal level. You'd never know, unless you had looked deep into his eyes.

And what of Mrs Connolly Senior? Well, back in Dundee, she went to the celebration party and together she and her son managed to put their disappointment on hold for a few hours. Helped, no doubt, by a glass or two of champagne and some good company.

# *Scott Crabbe*

On 3rd October 1992 Scott Crabbe signed for Dundee United from Heart of Midlothian Football Club. The United fans could hardly believe their good fortune to have secured the services of one of the finest and most respected players in Scotland. On March 1st 1994, Scott Crabbe broke his leg playing in the Scottish Cup replay against Motherwell at Fir Park. The United fans could hardly believe their misfortune. Scott Crabbe would not play in the final - if United made it to the final....

---

# NO MORE MR NICE GUY?

Scott Crabbe is one of the nicest guys in the game. Everyone says so. Hearts fans say it. United fans say it. Team-mates too. Even Hearts' manager, Joe Jordan, probably thought Scott Crabbe was a nice guy regardless of the fact that he put him on the transfer list. And it was no secret that Crabbe never really wanted to leave the Tynecastle club. He'd been with them for nine seasons, before that he'd been going to watch them with his father since he was six years old. When he signed for Hearts as a schoolboy it was, he says, the fulfilment of every fan's dreams - playing for the team he supports.

But the dream must have become something of a nightmare when the arrival of Joe Jordan at Tynecastle brought a change of direction in Crabbe's career. Suddenly the player, to the bewilderment of the player himself and the Tynecastle faithful, found himself surplus to requirements. The writing was on the wall when Jordan tried to sell him to St Johnstone.

Any player in Crabbe's situation could be forgiven for harbouring feelings of betrayal, anger and frustration. But not Scott Crabbe. It's not in his nature. Instead he resisted the urge to make a hasty departure from Edinburgh and simply waited for the kind of move that would suit him. When Jim McLean came in with a bid Scott Crabbe packed his bags and moved to Tayside. Back at Tynecastle the Hearts' fans scratched their heads and muttered dark oaths, up at Tannadice he was welcomed with open arms.

When he stepped into the arena against Aberdeen at Pittodrie everyone knew that Jim McLean was a wise man for Scott Crabbe was some mover.

Here was a player who had run a million miles or so for his former club who looked as though he would run a million more for United. A clever, selfless man who holds the midfield together and supports the players in front of him. Scott Crabbe can diagnose and exploit an opponent's next move - when he doesn't have the ball you can see him going off in search of it. And then he uses it as if he has a great affection for it. He seems to know where the ball is supposed to go and has that rare combination of adventurousness without being reckless. He rarely makes mistakes. Joe Jordan was obviously a very short-sighted man!

Ask Crabbe about the move to United and he'll say that of course it was a wrench for him to leave Hearts. But sometimes change can be beneficial. To experience different managerial styles, different training regimes and even the different philosophies which are adhered to in football can only be advantageous. And Crabbe has nothing but praise for Jim McLean. "He knew that coming to United was a big decision for me, but he has always been very understanding and has constantly encouraged me." Crabbe has no doubts that he has made the right move.

And one of the 'carrots' which might have been dangled before Crabbe as an enticement was the opportunity to win a trophy or two. Hearts hadn't procured any silverware since the late Fifties, United's record in that department was more encouraging and they always seemed to be there, or thereabouts, in the major competitions.

And just when United were looking like contenders for the Scottish Cup in 1994, Scott Crabbe goes and breaks his leg. An injury which was to keep him out of the game for nine months or more.

The game was Motherwell against United in the Cup replay at Fir Park. Brian Welsh had scored and, as Scott Crabbe set out on a run towards Sieb Dykstra in Motherwell's goal, the crowd held it's breath. Was this going to be goal number two? Would this ensure the win?

When he tumbled to the ground it looked as though he had merely winded himself, but it was soon apparent that it was serious. His leg was broken. Scott Crabbe was placed on a stretcher, a blanket draped over him and he was carried slowly towards the players' tunnel. There was much emotion in the United end of the ground. Some saw the ambulance arrive. Somehow it took much of the joy out of the eventual victory that night.

The player looks back to that fateful moment. "I didn't hear it break." he says, "People always ask if I heard it break, but I didn't. I was in great pain and I saw my leg flop, so I knew it was broken. I remember running in on goal, I'd had a bad touch on the ball and it was running away from me, so I stretched to get to it because I was thinking that here we were 1 0 up and if I could score, the game was over. When I collided with Dykstra – it wasn't even a bad challenge – but within seconds both he and I were pleading with the referee to get a doctor."

This was the first time Crabbe had been badly injured in his career. He'd pulled various muscles and been sidelined for a week or two, but when they told him in the hospital that it might be six months or more before he was back playing he could hardly believe it. Six months is a long time in football, especially when Crabbe believes he had reached his best form with United. "It had been hard for me to hold down a place with so many other good players around, but I'd had an unbroken run of about ten games before that night and felt I was playing quite well."

And, of course, he would miss the Cup final. "Naturally I would have liked to have played in such an important game, I would have loved to have pulled on a strip and run out there with the others." he says but with typical modesty adds, "But it wasn't to be and maybe if I had been playing we might have lost. And wouldn't that have been awful? The team that won the Cup was outstanding, the selection was exactly right - who knows what might have happened if those of us who weren't selected had played, it could have been disastrous. Individual ambitions had to take second place to collective effort."

And he cites the cases of David Narey and Paul Hegarty. "How could I gripe about not getting a chance to play in this game when there were guys like that who deserved a medal more than I did. I shared a room with David Narey in East Kilbride and he was so desperate for the boys to go out and do it this time, and when they handed him the trophy on the pitch I thought it was a particularly emotional moment."

And Ivan Golac's contribution? "The gaffer is superb. He sends you out thinking you're the best player in the world - better than the guy you're playing against. He doesn't mind if you make a mistake - so you're in a relaxed frame of mind. He made me feel very much a part of the whole build-up to the game. His speech to the players on the Friday night was brilliant. He told them that this was a chance to make history and you could see them sitting up and taking notice. I just thought at the time, these boys are going to go for it."

And Golac involved him in everything, he even brought him to sit on the bench. "I was right in the thick of things, and even if I don't get another chance to be in a Cup winning side, this was such a special occasion I enjoyed it almost as much as I would have done if I'd been part of the team."

And what of his recovery? "This has been such a long haul for me - I'm itching to get back, but I realise that it's going to be hard to try to be the same kind of player after this. It'll be like starting my career all over again. Just kicking the ball is painful at the moment and I'll probably be wary of tackles for a wee while. I suppose I'll have to be a little harder."

No more Mr Nice Guy? Somehow, I doubt it.

## *Dan Dailly*

Dan Dailly is a taxi driver. He also runs a small hotel and has spells as a debt counsellor and loan arranger. Actually he's a civil engineer but when you have a family of five you find yourself wearing many different hats. And Dan isn't even his real name. He was christened Alistair but at school was nicknamed Dan after the American movie star of that name – and the name has stuck. He is, of course, Christian's father.

---

# A PARENT'S PRAYER

If my lovely wife, Arlene, is correct in her assertion that football is a drug, then I have to hold up my hands and admit to being a junkie. After years of denial, I now confess to occasionally employing devious tactics to get my fix and, indeed, to suffering from 'cold turkey' (no reflection on Arlene's cooking!) during the close season. However, I'm delighted to announce that Arlene's rehabilitation programme, which included a season ticket for Dens Park, is now paying dividends and, to date, I have managed to kick the habit on Friday evenings, other than when there are Reserve League fixtures, and have resisted using the aforementioned season ticket, other than for local derbies.

Although she doesn't agree, I feel that her contribution to my addiction cannot be discounted insofar as she played a very major part in the production of our five children, three of whom are male and play football! It goes without saying that the other two are female and I should like to take this opportunity to kill off the myth that either play for the Scottish Ladies Football Team, as per past Press reports.

For the record, Victoria is nine and pretty tangerine behind the ears as far as her knowledge of football is concerned. I'm sure she thinks that boys don't work when they leave school, they just become professional footballers. Stefani, however, is fifteen and a fully paid up member of the Teeny Tangerine Terrors Club. She is the football statistician of the family and anything she doesn't know about every player's age, eye colour, hairstyle, vital statistics, etc is not worth knowing about.

Without doubt, Christian and his two younger brothers, Marcus and Kirk, are my reason or, more accurately, my main excuse for dedicating so much of my spare time to football over the years and, although I have always viewed this devotion to duty as a sacrifice, Arlene remains convinced that it is an addiction. Whether devotion or addiction, the fact of the matter is that I have loved every minute of it.

Christian requires no introduction but I should like to take this opportunity to introduce you to his brothers. Marcus is eighteen and, after a brief spell as an apprentice at Tannadice, now plays for (whisper it!) Dundee Football Club. Kirk, on the other hand, is just eleven and is Sporting Club 1990 FC's answer to Andrei Kanchelskis, at least that's how he sees it. Personally speaking, I feel that the comparison is not without justification, albeit he doesn't possess the pace, skill, vision or finishing power of Andrei! As the Manager of Sporting Club, which incidentally is the club Christian played for as a boy, I feel that I am reasonably well placed to make that judgement. If drawn into making a comparison, I would probably tend to go for Walter Carlyle, which begs the question – whatever happened to Walter? If he is fortunate enough to read this book, perhaps he would like to know that he is fondly remembered by those who not only support Dundee United but also support grey hairs.

Talking of grey hairs, I am absolutely convinced that the vast majority of mine are attributable to the fact that I both support and manage football teams. Quite frankly, the anxieties, traumas and emotions associated with these pastimes do not bear thinking about, as many of you will appreciate. What some may not appreciate, however, are the stress and emotional levels associated with being both a supporter and a parent. Ever since Christian broke into Dundee United's first team as a 16 year-old, I have been on a real emotional roller coaster although, to be fair, the ride has given me many highs including his Premier League debut and first League goal against St. Johnstone at 16, his first U/21 International Cap at 16, the 'phone call from Andy Roxburgh to say that he was included in the full International squad for the games against Estonia, his 'B' International Cap against Wales, etc. Unfortunately, a football roller coaster always has its fair share of lows and, from a personal point of view, I recall the long periods of absence through injury and the periods when he was under attack from sections of the crowd as being the most depressing. The two seasons during which he suffered problems with his knees and had to undergo surgery on four occasions were undoubtedly the most traumatic. I can assure you that watching your son playing on his return after surgery is almost guaranteed to have a major impact on the colour of your hair. Comments from the crowd, whether complimentary or derogatory, are part and parcel of the game and, as a supporter, I accept the old adage that 'you must take the bad with the good'. As a parent, I accept the fact that life on a Saturday afternoon is not always going to be a bed of roses and that my family and I may have to endure Christian being on the receiving end of a few verbal unpleasantries. However, like all relations of players who find themselves in that situation, I make sure that I always carry the standard survival kit, ie a coat of thick skin, a lip button and a pair of rubber ears. With that in mind, the next time you attend a match and are bored with the action (United leading by seven goals!), you may want to entice your son or daughter to play a game of 'Spot the Relative'. I'll give you another clue – we're usually ashen white and congregating in or around the freebie seats.

I am sure that I speak for all the players' parents and wives when I say that every game leaves you emotionally drained. However, at the start of Cup final week, I suddenly had this awareness of entering unexplored territories. On the one hand, I revelled in the air of optimism which prevailed amongst the United supporters but, on the other hand, I wanted to lock the event somewhere in the back of my mind until the Saturday, but the media hype and the ongoing banter between friends ensured that this was an impossibility. I was suffering all the emotions of a supporter who had experienced the six previous failures but, in addition, all the emotions associated with being personally involved in a paternal sense. Being the eternal pessimist, most of my thoughts concentrated on dealing with the disappointment of failure, not only on behalf of myself but also my family, particularly young Kirk whom I knew would be devastated if he had to attend another wake at 4.45 pm on Saturday, 21st May 1994. On the more positive side, I clung to the hope that the law of averages theory would at last come up trumps and the fact that my lucky number is seven. My dreams of victory tended not to concentrate on Christian collecting his Winners' medal and holding up the Scottish Cup but on the fact that he stood on the threshold of being part of Dundee United's folklore. Like most Dundee United supporters who are old enough to remember the 1960 promotion winning side, I can still rattle off the players' names like the Lord's Prayer; likewise United's Championship winning side of 1983 and, God forbid, Dundee's Championship winning side of 1963. (Of course, they only won the First Division Championship whilst we won the Premier League Championship.) Above all, that was the sort of status I hoped Christian could achieve through victory on the Saturday.

Actually, I had another two Cup finals to contend with immediately prior to the Cup final and, whilst they may have provided a welcome distraction from the main event, they offered little in the way of relaxation. Indeed, before or during these finals, the only part of my anatomy which enjoyed a relaxed state was my bowel! Kirk was performing in both, one with

Sporting Club and the other with his Primary School team, Downfield, and I was doing the Ivan Golac bit. Quite naturally, as a part of our pre-match build up, we had a leisurely stroll in the park, collecting wild flowers and making daisy chains.

In my mind, I tried to prioritise the three finals and gauge my emotional state in the event of any one of the numerous combinations of victories and defeats. Three victories and I'd hit the jackpot, three defeats and I'd probably hit the bottle! The very fact that victory for Dundee United would constitute history in the making simplified the prioritisation exercise – above all, I wanted victory for United, with victories in the other finals being a very welcome bonus. As it turned out, Sporting Club scored a victory whilst Downfield were very unlucky to lose after a penalty shootout. (By the way, referring back to my earlier comparison between Kirk and Andrei, I omitted to mention that Andrei is also slightly better at taking penalties!) Actually, on facing fourteen distraught Downfield schoolboys in the dressingroom after the shootout, I began to wonder if, in fact, I had got my priorities right.

Surprisingly, despite the relentless attention of the media and wellwishers, Christian gave the impression of being very relaxed and taking it all in his stride. Indeed, any stranger visiting the house would probably have thought that I was the one going under the microscope at Hampden Park on Saturday – well, any stranger with a white stick! The week flew by and, come the Thursday morning, Christian packed his bags, gave his Mum the customary peck on the cheek and headed West, leaving behind an unmade bed and the all-too-familiar trail of dirty undies, socks, tee-shirts, etc stretching from his bedroom to the washing machine.

For me, it was work as usual on the Friday but there was nowhere to hide as far as the Cup final was concerned. Even travelling to and from work, the game was analysed and re-analysed in typical Jimmy 'the Chin' Hill fashion by my passengers, 'Double K', 'Hissing Sid' and 'The Mighty Quinn', whilst at the office, the subject of the Cup Final was never far from the lips of all the staff and, with the exception of the odd 'Teddy Bear', they were all hoping for and, indeed, confident of, a United victory. I was my usual cautious self, not wanting to tempt fate by agreeing with the majority viewpoint as, deep down inside, I was still praying for a minor miracle. However, on Friday Sportscene, the self-confessed miracle man and footballing Messiah, Ivan Golac, appeared before the multitudes with promises of taking his Tangerine Army to the Promised Land and all negative thoughts were, at least temporarily, dispelled from my mind.

On the Saturday, my legion awoke early and assembled their weapons – scarves, tammies, flags, etc. Marcus had volunteered for the advance party and left on the Friday evening to check out some of the local hostelries – I mean hostilities! Victoria and Granny Dailly had, somewhat reluctantly, agreed to stay behind and look after our domestic affairs, particularly the video recording of the game. At the age of seventy-nine, Granny couldn't really be trusted with modern technology and consequently Victoria, at the tender age of nine, was entrusted with the responsibility for recording the pre-match build-up on one four hour tape before switching to another tape at 2.30 pm for the big game.

Just as we were about to depart, the 'phone rang and it was my brother's son, Clinton, reporting that the unthinkable had happened – he had lost his Cup final ticket! He obviously appreciated that he was asking the impossible but, nevertheless, I made a few 'phone calls, including one to Christian at his hotel, but it transpired that he <u>was</u> asking the impossible. Rather sadly, all I could do was report back and suggest that either he watch the game on the box or joined the Army in the hope that he could pick up a ticket at Hampden. Obviously, the latter option was likely to leave him savouring the atmosphere of the final from the Hampden Car Park.

However, at 10.00 am we finally slipped into the stream of cars, buses, mini-buses and vans on the A90 and joined Ivan's Tangerine Army on the road to Hampden. Stefani and Kirk secured their scarves such that they trailed out of the windows on both sides of the car, as our contribution to the sea of tangerine and black in the procession. Memories flooded back of the same journey in 1991 and, particularly, of how all our confidence and optimism turned to total despair on the way back. I still remember that return journey and, in particular, a tiny abandoned tangerine teddy lying at the roadside, about 5 miles from Perth. Strangely enough, Arlene referred to that same teddy when we were overtaken by a car, proudly bearing a large tangerine teddy on the roof. It may sound a bit childish but I remember thinking that it looked quite defiant – ready to take on the blue bears! Judging by all the happy smiling faces in the procession and all the scarves, banners and flags on display, I think we were all ready to take on the 'Teddy Bears'.

I had decided to park at the Rangers end of Hampden and, consequently, I slipped out of the tangerine procession and into the barely noticeable blue one as we passed through Glasgow. This decision was based on a combination of confidence and logic – after we won the Cup, the Blue Army would make a hasty and ignominious retreat, thereby facilitating our victorious return to Dundee through the deserted, conquered territories of Glasgow!

When we arrived at Hampden, the Tangerine Army had started to gather outside the main entrance, to await the arrival of Field Marshall Golac and his young Lieutenants. For the first time that day, I started feeling a bit nervous and apprehensive, probably because, up to that point, my mind had been preoccupied with the general arrangements and the journey. However, Sergeant Smith and his highly paid mercenaries appeared on the horizon and there was a general jockeying for position as the members of the Tangerine Army battled for the vantage points, not because they wanted the best view but because they wanted to ensure that the Rangers players were within earshot. Rather naively, I assumed that, being the proud possessors of a European Fair Play Award, they wanted to convey their kindest regards and best wishes for the final. Surprise, surprise – Walter's shell-shocked soldiers were obliged to run for the cover of Hampden, with only the odd one stopping to lick Hugh Keevins' hairy lollipop in the passing, as the muted applause of the Blue Army was totally drowned out by the tribal war-like chants and dances coming from the Tangerine Army. Cries of 'Ivan Golac's Barmy Army' were ringing in their ears as they took to their heels. Only Big Fergie stopped to sign autographs and, periodically, I could see him glancing across at the awesome enemy with a look of sheer bewilderment. Although, at the time, I thought this was an act of defiance, I now believe that he was seriously considering desertion.

No sooner had the troops settled down, when the chanting and dancing started up again. The Popemobile had been spotted coming down the hill, shrouded in a tangerine halo. As Ivan and his foot soldiers disembarked, looking totally relaxed and taking time to wave and clap, the troops ran through their repertoire of tribal songs, including their current No. 1 hit – 'There's Only One Craigie Brewster', sung to the melody of 'Winter Wonderland'.

Joking aside, it was a very emotional time for me. When Christian emerged to receive the acclaim of the supporters, I had a lump in my throat and was very nearly reduced to tears. On two or three occasions that day, I was to sense that my emotions were getting the better of me but, for some reason, my eyes never filled up as I had anticipated, and this intrigued me. Some time later, I discussed this with Arlene and, strangely enough, she had undergone a similar experience – on what was one of the proudest and emotionally charged days of our lives, our tear-ducts were dry. We concluded that, subconsciously, we had detached ourselves, ever so slightly, from the events of the day, thereby ensuring that we never allowed ourselves to reach an emotional peak because falling to the depths of despair would have been too traumatic. Although the experience is difficult to explain, probably it could best be described as some sort of emotional cocoon.

I resisted the temptation to enter the ground too early, preferring to occupy both my time and my mind by mingling with the crowd and chatting to anyone who had an accommodating ear. This apparent reluctance to keep my date with destiny was specifically designed to ensure that I didn't become a nervous wreck before the game even kicked off, but it annoyed and frustrated both Stefani and Kirk who, being normal humanoids, were understandably desperate to savour the atmosphere <u>inside</u> the ground. However, Christian's girlfriend, Kirsty, arrived on the wives' bus and I had a blether with her before moving on to my neighbour, Bob Donaldson, and then to some of my old mates – 'Burnsie', 'Fish Fernie' and 'Bloss' – who no longer reside in the great City of Discovery but remain ardent Arabs. Indeed, we were in deep discussion about the good old days and the seconds were ticking away nicely when Arlene informed me that the time for procrastination was over as the kids were tearing their hair out. I bade my friends a fond farewell, took a deep breath and entered the arena. As they say – 'Cometh the hour, cometh the man'!

With the Philistines occupying every space on the West Bank and the Arabs occupying every space on the East Bank, my immediate impression was that the revamped Hampden Park looked something special. An artist commissioned to paint the scene could have afforded to be economical in his use of colours. With the tangerine of the Terrors and the royal blue of the Bears clearly demarking the respective occupied territories, only the green grass of the playing surface offered an alternative. The rival choral groups competed with each other as well as the Tannoy system and, needless to say, we were one up before the game had even started. In the past the United support would never have won a Gold Medal for 'Synchronised Singing' but, somehow, it all came together on the day. It was as if they knew that this was to be their day.

From my position in the South Stand, I surveyed the scene and found it all very touching. Everyone in tangerine and black looked so cheerful, confident and relaxed, a situation which I found hard to come to terms with as I was all screwed up inside. I was still travelling in hope and praying for the game to get underway. I recall that the release of the balloons (no, the 'Gers had not appeared on the park!) provided a bit of light relief and, in Arlene's opinion, possibly a significant pointer to the outcome of the match. The royal blue balloons were up and over the West Stand within seconds whilst, in sharp contrast, the tangerine and black balloons filled the air space over Hampden before dancing off to the sounds of the Barmy Army. Arlene suggested that this was an omen.

Although my ticker was thumping against my rib cage at the time, I was delighted to welcome the arrival of the players onto the park as it signalled the fact that the real action was imminent. Fortunately, Herr Farry's use of the goose-step ensured that the time taken for the formal introductions was kept to a minimum. Throughout, my eyes were firmly fixed on a very relaxed looking Christian and I felt very emotional and proud. Win or lose, this was the fulfilment of one of a father's dreams.

Strangely enough, when the whistle blew and the game got underway, I started to relax and enjoy the occasion. Christian's early touches were reasonably productive and, from a personal point of view, this was the next best thing to a tranquilliser. As often happens when you are enjoying yourself, the time flew by and before I knew it, we were off to join my sister and brother-in-law, Lesley and Ian, in the queue for a half-time cuppa. The general consensus of opinion was that the dream was now a reality. As fate would have it, there was an announcement to the effect that there was no tea or coffee because, of all things, they had run out of hot water. I think the Lord must have been behind us because the queue quickly evaporated before us, thereby accelerating our return to the action. No sooner had we settled back in our seats, than our prayers were answered.

> "Brewster rose like a bird and flicked the ball on; McPherson was in two minds but neither was that of a footballer; Dailly homed in on the hapless prey; Maxwell juggled with the pack but drew the Joker; Dailly glided past him and picked his spot; the ball rolled agonisingly along the line before striking the post and rebounding; the Tangerine Army held their breath; Brewster shuffled his feet; the World stopped revolving momentarily and then – Brewster rifled home!"

The fans went absolutely bananas! Arlene, Stefani, Kirk and I danced and gestured like imbeciles. Arlene and I hugged and kissed unashamedly. I considered repeating this with the gentleman sitting on my left hand side but then decided against it because I knew Arlene would be green with envy. When all the animals had settled back in their cages, I checked my pulse to make sure that I was still alive. When checking my pulse, I glanced at my watch and thought, "Why the bloody hell can't we score the winner in the last minute!" My mind raced back to the previous Rangers match when we took an early second half lead and I prayed that history wasn't about to repeat itself. I decided not to look at my watch again because I knew that the hands would be turning anti-clockwise. I returned to my cocoon and tried to switch off mentally but it proved an impossibility. Suffice to say, for me the remainder of the game was sheer hell!

After the most agonising 40 minutes I have ever experienced, the final whistle finally blew and the 'Final Hurdle' had been finally hurdled. I jumped out of my seat, my head just missing the steel girders on the roof of the South Stand, before hugging and kissing anyone who was prepared to take me on, including Arlene. Significantly, the aforementioned gentleman on my left hand side had done a runner. As Ivan, the players, the wives and girlfriends, the Board of Directors and the supporters all joined in one big celebration party, I cried inside. My son, Christian, was now part of Dundee United folklore.

My thoughts turned to Jim McLean because, although he had failed to deliver on six occasions, this was his victory as much as anyone else's. He was Mr Dundee United and it might have been easy to forget that in all the euphoria after the final whistle.

However, the Messiah had delivered us to the Promised Land and, to him, I dedicate my Parent's Prayer:–

Our Father, which art in Heaven,

> Hallowed be the names of,
> Van de Kamp,
> Malpas, Petric and Welsh,
> Cleland, Bowman, Hannah and McInally,
> McLaren, Brewster and Dailly
> Also, Nixon and Bollan

**AMEN AND GOD BLESS DUNDEE UNITED**

## *Dougie Hope*

The best compliment you can pay any football referee is to say that you hardly noticed his presence during a game - and when Dougie Hope refereed the Scottish Cup final both sets of fans could have been forgiven for forgetting that he was there. It was fitting that this much-respected official was commissioned to oversee this game for, after 12 years as a Grade 1 referee, this was to be his swansong. Mind you, he still turns out to referee the odd game - at his local school.

---

# HOPE'S LAST BLAW

The build-up to the National Cup final starts months beforehand. Each referee or linesman is always desperate to be allocated to a Cup tie simply because it has this aura of excitement attached to it - and as the rounds go by the excitement gets greater. I refereed a number of ties in the earlier rounds which were good games and ones that supporters of both sides all seemed to enjoy.

I was informed by letter from the SFA that I was being appointed to the 1994 National Cup final - I was totally taken by surprise by this for a number of reasons. Firstly I had refereed a final two years previously - Rangers versus Airdrieonians. Secondly, I felt that there were a number of other referees who were as good as I was, if not better. And lastly, I was moving house when the letter came and so I had other things on my mind.

I think that it is fair to say that my family were more excited about this game than I was. My daughter, Lorna, who always went with me to all the games (not to support me, I suspect, but to see what the talent was like!) was so high she forgot all about the serious matter in hand - we were in the middle of moving house! My son, Graeme, who was not at my last final immediately set about the task of securing a ticket. My wife was not sure at that stage whether she would go or not. At the last final - her first ever football match - she was heard to say in the Stand, "It goes much faster on television!"

As a result of my being appointed to the Cup final the Glasgow Association of Referees, of which I am a member, presented me with the New Zealand Plaque. This plaque was given to the Glasgow Association by the New Zealand Referees' Association as a thank-you for the friendship extended by Scottish referees to their New Zealand counterparts during the last world war. Since then the plaque has been presented every year to the Cup final referee along with a New Zealand dollar which he keeps.

To have my name inscribed on the plaque once is tremendous, but twice is something else, particularly when you see some of the names - Jack Mowat, Bobby Davidson, Tom Wharton, William Syme and his son, David, Brian McGinlay, Ian Foote - and my own brother, Kenneth Hope. Having two sons who have been appointed to the Scottish Cup final brought tremendous joy to my Mum and Dad, who are both now eighty years of age.

The build-up to the Cup final really gets into gear immediately after the semi-finals take place. The press want various stories and photographs - in some of the photos my Jack Russell dog was the star attraction! Mind you, I didn't really start thinking about the game until probably about three or four days beforehand. Up until then there were other games to be refereed - some maybe not quite as glamorous but nonetheless to the players involved they were every bit as important. One such game was between St Cuthbert Wanderers and Wigtown and Bladnock at Kirkcudbright. I remember it well, not because it was a great game, or because there was any trouble, but for two other aspects, one being the beautiful setting and the surrounding scenery - the ground was next to the river. The other was the crowd - there were not many there, fifty or so - and you could hear the responses to my decisions. In the main they were well received, but having given one which they felt inclined to disagree with, one wag shouted, "Next time you do that you're in the river." Quick as a flash I replied. "I can swim." Back came the answer, "No wi' two bricks roon yer neck!".

At the end of that game some of the crowd came to shake my hand and thank me for coming. Now that's what football is all about!

The evening prior to the Cup final seemed no different for me to any other Friday evening. However on this occasion I was quickly brought out of any daydreaming by a telephone call that I made to my fellow referee, James Herald. He wasn't at home so I chatted to his wife, Joan, who I know well. At the end of the conversation she asked me if I was going to the game the following day. It was then that it dawned on me that I really had to go. What she said really brought it home to me - some say it's only a game, but this was an important one.

On the Saturday morning, like most other mornings, I was up around 7.00am to take the dog out for a walk - and I was soon accosted by the milk boys and the paper boy who all wanted to stop for a chat about the game and speculate about who was going to win. One boy questioned my sanity in getting up so early on Cup final day, he reckoned that I would be knackered by the time 3.00pm arrived.

After having breakfast and a wash and a shave my daughter ran me into Glasgow where I was meeting one of my linesmen, Donald McVicar, and a few other referees. Donald and I had decided that we would meet for a cup of coffee and a leisurely chat, however all that went out the window because he brought along two other refs - Ray Morrison and Hugh Dallas, so the five of us (my daughter decided to stay as well) had a good laugh, but what really surprised us was that Ray Morrison bought the coffee!

Having recovered from the shock of Ray buying the coffee Donald and I were driven to the Moat House Hotel where we were to be the guests of the supervisors for lunch (three courses and I ate every one!). After the hearty meal we were driven to the ground in two cars (Donald and I in one and Graeme Alison, the other linesman, and the fourth official, Dr Death - Andrew Waddell, in the other). On arrival there were the usual requests for interviews for both television and radio.

When we inspected the playing surface we discovered that the TV cameras were attached to the goalposts at either end. At one end one worked while at the other the other one did not. The TV company later discovered tape over the lens. Now who would do such a thing?

Prior to the immediate commencement of the game introductions to a number of dignitaries were carried out. The principle guest was Ian Lang, the Secretary of State for Scotland (who, incidentally, is my boss!). It is almost impossible to hear what is being said because of the tremendous noise from the crowd.

I felt that the ninety minutes flowed quite well, so much so that it seemed to me to have lasted only a few minutes - but my ribs told me otherwise, you see I was refereeing the game with three broken ribs, an injury which I sustained a few weeks earlier.

The presentation of medals is over before you know it and you are back in your changing room comparing medals and having a cup of tea (well it looks like tea!). One very nice touch was that Walter Smith, the Rangers' manager, presented me with a Cup final jersey and thanked me for refereeing over these past 12 seasons.

At the Referee's Summer Conference in St Andrews I discovered that as a result of having refereed the Cup final I got top marks from the supervisors for the season and I was presented with the Jack Mowat Trophy in front of

400 fellow referees - sadly Jack himself was not there, unfortunately he took ill the day before.

The Cup final was my last game and one of my colleagues wrote the following poem.

## DOUGIE'S LAST BLAW

For mony a season yi'v been able to see
wee Dougie Hope, the fitba' referee
Aroon' the park he'd strut his stuff
blawin' his whistle if things got rough

Sma' but wiry and a wee bit crabbit
the wee legs noo are gettin' wabbit
The once bright eyes are gettin' dimmer
soon be time tae get a zimmer

First tae arrive each week at trainin'
last tae git oot, the nights it's rainin'
Thinks up things tae keep ye fit
the nasty wee sadistic git

Remembers well wan fateful day
the immortal words o' auld John Gray
"A'm fed up wi' you takin' a' these names
find another mug to gie you games"

This he did and for mony years
became the favourite o' Matty Spiers
Ayrshire's gain was the Central's loss
as Dougie showed 'em wha was boss

Seasons passed, he wis dae'n jist fine
got promoted tae runnin' the line
Went tae twa as quick as ye can
and then he made it tae Class wan

Even then, he'd no long tae wait
making FIFA in eighty-eight
Foreign appointments he didnae lack
but efter each gemme they'd send him back

In the last few years he stole the show
dae'n Rangers Celtic three gemmes in a row
While some said great, others wid laugh
did he no ken efter a goal ye go back to yer ain half

Four finals in the last three years
puts him up beside his peers
So be nice to Dougie if yer really wise
he jist might be back tae supervise

So if ye wonder how the South will cope
without the wee man, Dougie Hope
Dinnae worry, dinnae stress
we might no always be Hope-less

## *Billy Kay*

His is a weel-kent face, not only on the slopes of Tannadice but also to wider audiences, for Billy Kay is a writer, broadcaster, historian, raconteur and connoisseur of fine wine. His love of the Scots language manifests itself in all his work. Born in Ayrshire he has now made Newport-on-Tay his home and much of his writing has been concerned with Dundee and its people.

# TALES OF ARABIAN KNIGHTS

### THE DAYS WE DIDNAE WIN THE CUP

There remains little or no record of the days we didnae win the Cup. Very occasionally, ancient Arabs, puggled wi' the efforts of their day, will play a much-taped-over video and feel vague unease to find a five second remnant in claret and amber, white and black, green and white and royal blue - something from the distant past. The colours play on their subconscious, but are too painful to bring to the conscious self. Life goes on after all, and every year brings the prospect of a new jihad.

### MEMORIES OF THE RUN UP TO THE DAY WE WON THE CUP

The fantastic United support at Motherwell and big Welshie's goal; discussing 18th Century Scottish history with Chris Whatley at Broomfield; getting a letter from Gwen McIlroy asking me to contribute to a book about the day we would win the Cup - hey, the lassie's no aw there, was my immediate reaction - so I had nae problem sayin I would contribute; the blizzard and the fresh-baked bridie brocht fae Forfar by Graeme at the first semi-final, and devoured by health-conscious Dennis and me; Andy McLaren dead on his feet, yet orchestrating the support with five minutes to go against the Dons - never say die till y're deid - that's what got us the equaliser. Thanks again, Welshie. I missed the replay but became the founder member of the Blue Ridge Mountain branch of the Dundee United Supporters' Association. I reckon that when McInally's winner went in I was recording an Appalachian fiddler playing 'Hop High Ladies', their version of 'Miss McLeod of Raasay.' I got the result in Charlotte, North Carolina, two days later. All we needed now was Rangers in the final, Killie would present 'heid soartin' oot' problems for the club - the Gers we would just get torn intae. The referee obliged as usual. (Question: Which teams are awarded 'goals' like Hateley's against Kilmarnock? Answer: England in World Cup finals at Wembley and Rangers anytime, anywhere as long as it's a Scottish referee.)

Now it's hard to be humorous about Rangers, unless your sense of humour takes a distinctly black turn. I remember hearing a Gers fan at the World Cup final in Mexico wax lyrical on the difference between supporting Scotland and supporting the Teddy Bears: "When ye support Scotland, everybody's yer pal. Ye're friendly, ye have a good time, but when ye support Rangers ye hate everybody. Aw these Mexicans are great folk, great fun, but if I wes wi Rangers they would aw be Papish bastards an I'd hate them." And this from a reasonably intelligent Rangers fan. I've observed others rampage through the Hilltown in Dundee singing, "What's it like to f— a nun?", stick the heid on one another to celebrate a goal and give the fascist salute while singing God Save the Queen. None of this is attractive to a liberal, left-of-centre nationalist. It is also a lumpen expression of what the club stands for - all that is right-wing, sectarian, loyalist and unionist. A club which put the knife into the Hampden renovation project years ago for its own selfish reasons, which would ditch Scottish football in a flash if the English superclubs would have them. No, I do not like Rangers.

While I was in the States, I got word from the Final Hurdle, the wonderful United fanzine, asking if I would write something for a special Cup final edition. Given Rangers' 'Rule Britannia' mentality and recalling that United in Cup finals, like a certain Scottish patriot in campaigns against the Auld Enemy, had failed six times I wrote the following:

Dring Dring......... Dring Dring.

Hello, is that Robert the Bruce? This is the Final Hurdle here. We were wondering if you could write something witty and amusing for the troops to go out in our special Bannockburn edition. No a haill bundle o' laughs in the big set-piece confrontations so far, I agree, but the spirit of the troops is incredible, they keep wantin' tae have another go. They're right behind you. I mean it doesnae have to be totally funny. Yea, you can frame it as Right versus Might, Goodies versus Baddies, Beauty versus The Beast, Civilisation versus Barbarism, David versus Goliath, yea, Noble Egalitarian Caledonians defending wives, weans and freedom o' the homeland versus pillaging Huns waving foreign flags, chanting obscenities and standing to the right o' Ghengis Khan! That's a pretty fair assessment of what the two sides stand for, right enough, Robert. But could ye no work in a bit of humour tae - maybe somethin' aboot heidbangers fae the Orange Groves of Lanarkshire, or the wan aboot the posh waiter askin' their intellectual midfield general, Ferguson, "If sir cared for some ginger with his melon?" and him replying, "Naw, Ray Wilkins has already ordered us a boattle o' wine!". Just somethin' to lighten it up a wee bit? Naw? OK, nae funnies fae you then. Whit about a story tae galvanise us then, inspire us tae the victory the hail civilised world kens we deserve? A spider? Casting her web? I like it. Disnae ken defeat, great. How many times does she fail before she succeeds? It disnae matter, it's a legend! OK. Ye keep daein it until ye win. I agree. But listen, just for the Bannockburn edition, we'll fix the spider's failures at the same number as oor failures to defeat the enemy in major battles and tie in her success with our coming victory at Bannockburn. Great Rab. The troops will love it. This, and the new song, will do the trick. Haenae heard it? Well, it's no actually about you, Rab, it's about a 'seer' fae Serbia who, like yer spider, prophesies victory. It goes: 'Ivan Golac's magic, he wears a magic hat...'

The first salvo was fired, it was now onward to Hampden. The cause was boosted by the news that the Gibson boay, unable to score a mini-bus for the troops, had hit upon the mould-breaking idea of calling a taxi firm and had succeeded in hiring a chauffeur-driven stretch limousine for the Cup final! With nine of us due to travel, it would maybe have to stretch a wee bit mair, but to travel in style like rich Arabs on the spree for the price of a train ticket tae Glesga appealed to us and definitely heightened our sense of anticipation for the big day.

## THE DAY WE WON THE CUP

Sitting on the railings at Tesco's car park watching the Arab legions go by in their buses, white United scarf with the narrow tangerine and black bands tastefully blended with the tangerine and black keffiyeh my daughter had been given by Final Hurdle editor, Steve, on her first appearance at Tannadice the week before. A good omen, the transport arrives on time - and what a sight, the stretch limo snooving round the corner bedecked with tangerine ribbons from prow to wing mirrors. The guests were off tae the waddin o' the century  - in style. (Title of United's Cup final history until now 'Six Funerals and a Waddin'?) Inside, the wily Desert Fox Gibson fae Newbiggin, his almond-eyed daughter and wife of many virtues, and Big Colin, son of the guardian of the Tannadice door, once of Fintry but now of Jeddah, here to join the jihad against the Orange Infidel, the Larkhaw Lumpen etc etc.

Big Dennis and Doctor Paul were squeezed aboard at Invergowrie, the car wes now hoatchin' wi' punters! With all Arabs blaming previous defeats for the way that they were dressed, Colin threw the limousine into intellectual and emotional turmoil by presenting us with genuine Arab kaffiyehs and eqals (the black circlets ye haud the kaffiyehs doun on the heid wi') - bought just a few days before in the souks of Jeddah. What a dilemma - the kaffiyehs were red and white - should they adorn the supporter's head, thus taking precedence over the tangerine and black United one? No oracles to consult, no precedents to guide us and the limo speeding ever closer to the jihad field of Mount Florida. The boays all donned their coiffes but the effect was not encouraging - they looked as though they had bought them in What Every Arab Wants - aw ower the place they were. Then, like a revelation, the solution appeared - remove the label/washin instructions/three year warranty or whatever from the eqals, and we became Mujahedeen fae Mecca, rather than Dung Scavengers fae Dundee. We were braw. Our stars were now high in the firmament, the pre-match champagne was tasting well and the growing sense of righteousness was confirmed when we discovered that the chauffeur was of the Tribe of Dens, fulfilling the allotted role of those unfortunate ones - by serving the Noble Tribe of Tannadice - the Terrors - on their Day of Total Triumph. We gathered at the flat of Dundee-exile, soul singer, Neil, in Glesga for the civilised lunch with chilled wine before the storm.

## THE GEMME

Was there ever a United support like thon? I did the samba with the Brazilian and Scots fans in Seville at the 1982 World Cup, but the carnival produced by the glorious 12,000 was every bit as electric. The team responded - McLaren and Dailly like greyhounds out of the slips, dictating a pace which was mesmerising the opposition. No goals though and no breaks from the referee. (Question: Would Rangers have got that penalty? Answer: DefinATELY!)

## THE GOAL THAT WON THE CUP

The Arab head-dress under the sun was hoat, but as things were going fine it could not be removed under any circumstances. Half-time then sent this Arab to the oasis at the back of the stand to slake his thirst. The crush at the toilets however took up the full ten minutes, the queue for the drinks was still enormous and the second-half had kicked off. Wi' a throat like a camel wi' the cauld, I headed back down to take up my position. I didn't get there. For, on my progress down, there occurred a strange and wonderful out-of-body experience in which I found myself taking off into the firmament - hovering in the air for many seconds with a feeling of ecstatic joy and landing among my tribe of celebrants two rows from the front. What caused it I shall never know. All I remember is Dailly running in on McPherson, Maxwell hitting the ball, Dailly recovering it and stroking it across the gaping maw of the goal, the frozen-in-time feeling when it hit the post and the tangering blur that was Brewster blootering it into the back of the net. It was at that second that I soared and dived like a desert falcon. All praise to the Gods - Muslim, Christian, Ivan and Brewster.

The rest of the second-half was sun-drenched and long as a desert afternoon. The Infidel attacked and attacked while the Arab legions howled to the heavens, sat stoically silent or danced and sang encouragement, depending on how many losing Cup finals they had attended. I was lucky. Possessing no timepiece, and separated from the Jeddah Brigade scattered all over Hampden's east slope, I presumed the suffering had still five minutes to run when the final whistle shrilled. Ode to Joy, Hymn of the Seventh Happiness, Desert Song of Elation. Twelve thoosan happy punters no kennin' whether tae greet or laugh, so daein baith at the same time!

A community swathed in tangerine, partying in the sun, warmed by the sight of our team doing the same - the players who had won the Cup, the rest of the squad who had contributed to the Cup run, the players who had given their all without success in the past - all joined together in a moment that will stay with us forever.


## SWEET MEMORIES OF THE AFTERMATH

Leaving Hampden and actually seeking out your pals from previous campaigns and celebrating with them instead of skulking out depressed, avoiding one another. Joining up with the Jeddah Brigade, we laughed all the way back to Neil's flat where the wonderful Michele, Honorary Capetown Arabesque, showing an optimism matched only by Ivan's, had actually baked a tangerine victory cake before the final whistle sounded! The royal progress in the stretch limo back to Dundee was exquisite; the camel watering oases of Steppes and Bridge of Earn where we drank victory cups and called our loved ones to share the joy o' thaim that bidit at hame. The luik on Dougie Donnelly's face as he tried to look neutral on the highlights at night.


## THE DAY AFTER WE WON THE CUP

The glow lasted and burst with pride as the family saw the Cup raised on the balcony in Dundee's City Square. It continued as I collected the redoubtable Minnie Way in Fintry and brought her home for a celebration tea. At 98 her last ambition had been achieved, her boys had won the Cup and brought it home 84 years since she had last seen it in her native city.

## THE WEEKS AND MONTHS AFTER WINNING THE CUP

My Portuguese Arabesque wife, João, and I scientifically calculated the sequence necessary for the aftermath glow to endure. Every week the videos should be shown in the following sequence on separate evenings:

1.    The Gemme

2.    The Highlights

3.    The Pre-gemme Build-up

Repeat until neat year's final when, hopefully, you'll have a new gemme to drool over.


## WISHES FOR THE TEAM THAT WON THE CUP

That the will to win, shown in the Cup run, implants itself in everyone's brain - banishing forever the cornershop mentality which limits ambition and holds back achievement.

That the club consolidates the skill in the squad by hiring quality international players and paying all the players the going rate for clubs challenging for European honours.

That Arabs banish dourness and support the players with pride and passion - even when things are going against them (remember three minutes to go in the first semi-final against Aberdeen!).

Finally, from every Dundee United supporter to the players who played in that magnificent Cup run, and that unforgettable final, THANKS FOR THE MEMORIES. You were just brilliant.

## *Sheila McFarlane*

Retired teacher and erstwhile company director, Sheila McFarlane, has been a dedicated United supporter for more years than she cares to remember. During the close season she spends much of her time travelling around the world and when, in November 1993, she booked a trip to China and realised that the departure date coincided with Scottish Cup final day she, and the travel agent (another United fan), laughed. United were having a poor season, there was no way that they'd make it to Hampden ...

---

# AIRPORT '94

At noon, 21st May 1994, I was dumped unceremoniously at Edinburgh Airport by a car full of gleeful Dundee United supporters, who were en route to Hampden. As my plane's take-off was scheduled for 5.00 pm, I had plenty of time to get organised and at least see the match on BBC TV. Loading the large case and overnight bag onto a trolley, I entered the building and was directed to a TV set in the lounge on the first floor. ("Back yourself into the lift and pull in the trolley," I was advised.)

The place was deserted, but I soon found a Good Samaritan to switch the television to the correct channel, chose the most comfortable chair, cleared a space for the luggage trolley and settled down to watch the run-up to THE GREAT MATCH. A short time later, a young man asked if he could join me in the prime position a few feet from the TV. It was quickly established that he was a fellow Dundee United supporter. (Richard Gough had appeared on the screen and my companion remarked "Judas.") He worked in London, could not get a ticket and, as the match was not being shown live in England, he had come up on the midday plane to Edinburgh and was returning after the game to collect, he was sure, all his winnings from his boozing pals – £300, he declared.

Having witnessed the six previous Cup finals, I expressed some misgivings – not about the team, but more about the refereeing standards in the Scottish game. An entertaining period followed, during which we classified the various 'whistlers' into the usual categories of BAD, WORSE and WORST. After some slight differences of opinion, we again gave our full attention to the TV screen as 3.00pm was fast approaching and the butterflies were having a field day in my stomach.

Tension mounted as the match started and the game progressed. The refusal of the official to give a penalty for the blatant foul on Alex Cleland made me heart-sick, but the way the team was playing had the pair of us smiling and not-so-quietly cheering in the now crowded lounge area. As half-time approached, I realised I would have to go and check in my luggage. As soon as the half-time whistle sounded, I rose, collected all my gear, left my 'luggageless' companion to his own devices, went back to the lift, reversed in, went down to the BA shuttle desk and presented my flight tickets, one to London and the other, London to Hong Kong. The girl at the desk slowly explained I would not have to collect my case in London and the next time I would see it would be in the Arrivals' area in Hong Kong. She then proceeded to ask the usual questions about whether I had packed my own suitcase, was I carrying any lethal weapons, explosives, electrical goods, gas cylinders and had I left my case unattended at any time or had anybody asked me to carry any boxes or parcels for them. Resisting the temptation to give some humorous answers, I asked her the one vital question, 'Is there a TV set in the shuttle lounge?' As her reply was in the affirmative, I rushed upstairs, but was pulled up short, as I had to place handbag and overnight bag on the X-ray machine and submit myself to the usual search. Free at last, I raced down the passage, only to find a well-filled lounge. Quickly spotting a seat, reasonably near to the screen, I sat down, but discovered the sound was so low, I could not hear Jock Brown's commentary on the second-half, which had already started. Who needed a commentary anyway, as long as I could SEE the game! That was until I noted at the foot of the screen, RANGERS 0 DUNDEE UNITED 1. Clutching feverishly at the arm of the person next to me, I asked, "Who scored?" When no reply was forthcoming, I turned and found myself looking into the inscrutable face of a Japanese gentleman, whose English wasn't good enough to produce a response. I then turned to the person on my left, but as she was reading a newspaper, I knew I would have to wait for the action replay of the goal. But the action replay crew must have still been at the Bovril and pies, because the goal never appeared. I sweated out the rest of the half, the last five minutes with hands over face, with just tiny chinks between the fingers showing the last and final long seconds of the game. At the final whistle, I gave the Cup Winners a standing ovation, clapping and shouting, "Well done, lads!" I think the room must have been full of foreigners and Rangers' supporters, for I found I was a lone voice! A minute or two later, the flight was called and all passengers started leaving, except me and my London companion, who had by now rejoined me and had started describing, in great detail, THE GOAL!

We were last to board the plane, as we tried to see as much of the celebrations and interviews as possible. We were unable to see the actual presentation of the Cup, but we certainly enjoyed the short flight to London. My, by now, slightly inebriated companion left me to go and collect his winnings and later while having dinner on the long flight out East, I toasted Dundee United Football Club with a few celebratory glasses of my favourite sparkling wine and hoped to be having a few more on our journeys back from the European games to be played in the near future.

*Gwen McIlroy*

Born in Belfast, Gwen McIlroy came to Scotland in 1974. She studied History and Politics at Edinburgh University and is the author of A VIEW FROM THE GROUND, a look at a season in the Scottish Premier Division through the eyes of a Dundee United fan. Having rashly announced that if United won the Scottish Cup she would produce a book about it, Gwen was probably the only United fan who turned up at Hampden worried that they might just go out and do it!

---

# OF GOALIES AND GHOSTIES ...
# AND THINGS THAT GO BUMP IN THE NET

"We're into the final", yelled the stranger who kissed me and clasped me to him like someone he had thought to be long-since dead when Jim McInally (God bless him) scooped the ball into the Aberdeen net in the semi-final replay. "We're on our way back to Hampden." sang the crowd. "We're on our way back to Europe." I thought.

And sure enough, we were. Again. And sometimes in the intervening weeks I wanted someone pinch me, for I just couldn't quite believe it. It had, you see, been an awful season. The worst that I can remember since I started to follow United way back in 1980. And yet, ironically it had been rescued by this tie against Rangers. The sense of joy (and relief) was overwhelming - until you thought of the enormity of it all.

And suddenly Mark Hateley started to haunt me. I only had to close my eyes and there he was - Footballer of the Year - running, unattended, towards some helplessly-mesmerized goalkeeper. Images of Ally McCoist and Gordon Durie also tended to have me tossing and turning in the wee small hours. When in full-frontal attack the Rangers firing squad would have sent a frisson down the backs of even the most lionhearted of United's fans. Très formidable. As Eric Cantona might say.

And now that you come to mention it, Walter Smith's ensemble held one or two other ghosts. There was a certain Ian Ferguson who, in his previous incarnation as a St Mirren midfielder (then boyish with his hair fashionably streaked), scored the only, and consequently winning, goal against the Tannadice side in the 1987 Cup final. Now that's the stuff of recurring nightmares! And let's not forget the former Motherwellian goalkeeper, one Alastair Maxwell, who stood heroically in situ in that tremendous 1991 final fending off many of United's advances despite having sustained a serious injury early on in the game.

And then, of course, there was Hampden itself. The Mecca of Scottish football - a field of memories and dreams, but for United it was the place where hopes were shattered and most of the memories best forgotten. There lurked the ghosts of Cup finals past. It's not that Dundee United have never won at Hampden, it's just that six fruitless Scottish Cup journeys home from Mount Florida made it seem so. But there was always the hope that now that the once-decaying and dilapidated arena had been refurbished, the phantoms and demons would have been vanquished with the cobwebs, and you held onto the belief that this would be the beginning of a new era for United. Exorcism at 3.00pm on May 21st or just a whole new Hampden hoodoo?

Other factors preyed on your mind. When Scott Crabbe was ruled out of the game because of injury it was a bitter blow. And then when Billy McKinlay was lost to the midfield every Ibroxologist in the land confidently predicted that the Cup was on its way back to Govan.

All in all, it looked as though there was not a lot going for United. However, there was an unmistakable air of optimism in the United camp. United's name, they said, was on the Cup. They felt it in their water. They'd tell you that where this competition was concerned Ivan Golac, unlike his predecessor, carried a modicum of luck. Brave words.

Seventh time lucky? How I longed that it would be so. The thought of defeat was unbearable. I remembered, all too vividly, the pain and grief of losing - and all the tears. The funereal silence of the journey home, and the endless post-mortems conducted up and down the land. I remembered, too, the immediate numbness and the residual ache that hurt and incapacitated for months afterwards. Years even. United the also-rans. United the perennial runners-up.

And yet, for all that, I wouldn't have missed it for the world. And anyway, in true Pythonesque fashion my inclination is to always look on the bright side of life. Deep inside me I knew that Rangers weren't quite as invincible as they, and their entourage, would have had us believe. They may again have been reigning champions of the Premier Division, but their season had been liberally peppered and punctuated with defeat (most notable perhaps, United's 3 - 0 victory at Ibrox before Christmas). Then again, would they perhaps be like some wounded animal - angry and more dangerous as a result? All the while I kept telling myself - it could be done. Their defence was decidedly creaky, and they were definitely in the throes of a goalkeeping crisis. While Ivan Golac, on the other hand, had in Gordan Petric, Brian Welsh, Maurice Malpas, Alex Cleland and Christian Dailly (yes, I did say, Christian Dailly) a wealth of stout defensive men from which to chose. Metaphorically speaking. And when it came to goalkeeping, my money was on Guido Van de Kamp.

And to tell the truth, I didn't care how United won. Fair means or foul. I wasn't perturbed whether it was a good game or not. I know what it's like to see your team play superb football and lose. Been there. Done that. Bought the bloody T-shirt! I didn't care a jot or a fig if the ball was lofted high and long for interminable periods and the watching nation bemoaned the passing of the passing game. I didn't even care how United·scored just so long as they did - offside strikes, undetected hand-balls, opposition own-goals, deflections off stray dogs/match officials/ball-boys/passing programme sellers, all gratefully received. I wouldn't even have complained if United had scored in the first minute and we had to endure 89 minutes of sheer hell before the Cup was secured. That kind of suffering makes winning all more sublime.

I even thought of taking a hand in the proceedings myself. I contemplated the Faustian approach - offering to sell my soul to the devil to secure victory, or conversely, taking to religion in my hour (and a half) of need. Or if, perchance, I should have happened upon the Rangers team bus en route to the match I would have felt duty-bound to drive, kamikaze-like, headlong into it. And if my nerve had failed me in that venture I could always have introduced a touch of salmonella to their pre-match meal. I even considered bribing the match officials (surprisingly no-one seemed to know the modern-day equivalent of 30 pieces of silver). I thought we could have had a whip-round and presented Douglas Hope and his sidekicks with a wad of used fivers in a brown envelope. Hard cash, I thought, might just do the trick.

In my calmer moments, however, I knew that I just had to trust the team and believe that if they played to their potential all would be well.

But if you want the truth, the whole truth and nothing but the truth this game was very much a watershed in my relationship with Dundee United or, to be more precise, with Dundee United's fans.

Going to watch United has become away of life for me. I felt very much at home at Tannadice. I loved the relaxed atmosphere and the genuine sporting attitude of the fans. There seemed to me to be a real appreciation of football on the terraces, win or lose the fans were good-natured and stoic, a fact which was universally recognised by FIFA's Fair Play Award after the 1987 UEFA Cup final when, after watching their team lose, the terraces rose to salute the winners, Gothenburg. This was a proud moment for both the club and its supporters, a genuinely moving experience. But times have changed. Drastically so, and I was no longer comfortable, for there had emerged a new breed of fan whose blinkered attitude made him (and, I have to say, it is largely a male failing) hate other teams with a vengeance, and despise his own when they weren't winning. I disliked those with tunnel-vision who saw only one team emerge at 3.00pm and who almost frothed at the mouth with anger and frustration. Where had all the joy gone?

On the field, the Premier Division was becoming stultified and the terraces seemed to be permeated with nothing but gloating, goading and bitterness. Clearly Scottish football was in the doldrums and the lean/crap/transitional patch which United were going through had brought the worst out in some of the fans, but when they started to turn on the players it was then that I really began to question whether I wanted to sit or stand beside, behind or in front, of people who could shout obscenities at the likes of Christian Dailly and Paddy Connolly. I have never once thought that a player has not tried to win a game. I have never once believed that a player has 'cost' us a match. There are no guarantees in football - it's a game partly based on mistakes - if no-one made a mistake then there would be no goals. I was tired of listening to sermons and dissertations from fans who couldn't kick a football to save their lives!

This game was, then, very much a test of the fans for me. I was scared that had it all gone wrong they would have been quick to turn on the team and that the psychological effect of this, and losing, would not have just lasted through the summer but would have proved so disastrous that it might well have crippled the club for years.

I began to prepare myself mentally for whatever the day would bring. I thought that if I could 'distance' myself from it all I would survive. So while others were announcing to all and sundry that United were going to win the Cup, I just couldn't bring myself to say it. Err on the side of caution, became my motto. When asked, I tended to mumble something about how I thought that maybe United wouldn't win. When pressed, I'm afraid I stated that I didn't think United had a prayer. Oh me of little faith. The closer we got to the final the louder I said it. I even said it on radio and in print. (I firmly believe that the BBC and most Scottish newspapers each have a file marked 'Dundee United Loony'. I am proud to announce I am that loony. Each time that United make headline news someone reaches for the file and I receive a phone-call.) In the week prior to the final I was

**McLaren & Hannah race to meet the ball**

Cleland heads clear

**Petric clears from Mikhailitchenko**

The Final Whistle. Malpas, Welsh & Petric celebrate

McLaren. We're gonna celebrate - with Lucozade?

All the eights. Hannah commiserates with Ian Ferguson

It was the wigs that did it!

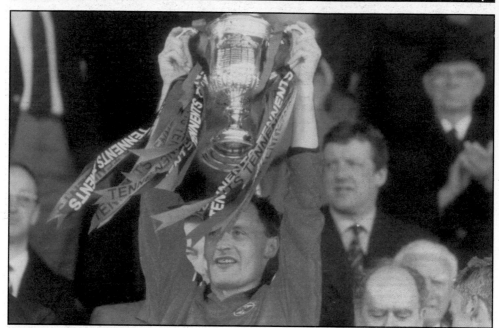

Golac salutes the crowd (Peace, Man!)

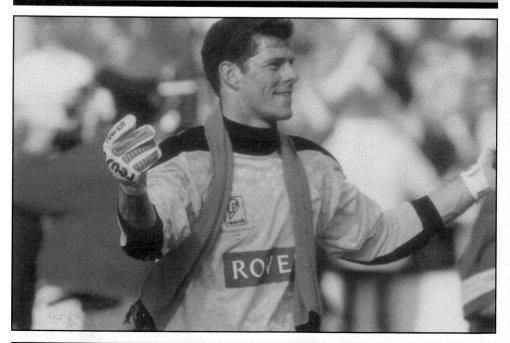

**Brewster stands before the fans**

Ivan Golac's magic hat

interviewed several times about whether or not United would win the Cup. Afraid of the suggestion that mine was a Utopian dream, I tended to prevaricate. Many of those who interviewed me openly laughed at United's chances of winning the Cup, they were probably still laughing when the game began. I doubt if they were laughing when the game ended.

Here and now I would like to make an apology to all the players, to Ivan Golac and to Jim McLean. Forgive me. Like all forms of denial, it was a means of defence. My rationale was simple, the more often I said I didn't think United would win the more I could protect myself from all the pain and heartache I knew I would experience in the wake of defeat. When people laughed and pointed their fingers and said, "Your team didn't win the Cup, I bet you were surprised." I could reply, "Not me. I knew they would lose. Ask anyone." Forgive me for my treacherous disloyalty. I wanted you to win so much.

Why, some might ask, was winning some old piece of silverware so important. Having thought long and hard about this, I have several explanations. For me, the world has become an increasingly bewildering place. A place where wars and famine rage, where hatred, greed and envy abound, where corruption prospers and the innocent and vulnerable are always victims. A place where wealth, enlightenment and common sense could eradicate much of the suffering but for the fact that the majority of us with lofty ideals are either too powerless, or too lazy, to do anything about these ills. Everyone needs a form of escape from such concerns. For me, football offers it. And the joy of being part of winning such an illustrious trophy lifts you out of the worry and mundanity of life in the late twentieth century. In many ways this game was symbolic, a microcosm of life. Victory was a triumph for the disadvantaged. Put quite simply, it was good fun. May 21st allowed us to experience such feelings of camaraderie and warmth that it made us believe that not everything in life is black (or blue!). For me it brought the restoration of much lost faith.

On another level, I so wanted United to win, not for myself, but for David Bowman. I love David Bowman. There, I've said it. He is one of the kindest, most thoughtful men I have ever met. I knew how much this trophy meant to him. He once told me that if United lost this final he was determined to lift the Cup when he went up to collect his runner's-up medal. He felt it might be his only chance to get his hands on it. Like Helen, his wife, (who loves him even more than I do!) I just wanted to see his face when he won it. I was, I have to say, richly rewarded.

Now, despite all my misgivings about this game, a funny thing happened on the way to the stadium. Slowly, inexplicably, I began to get the feeling that all would be well. Maybe, just maybe, United could pull it off. By the time I had reached the ground 'We're gonna win the Cup' had become my anthem.

I was one of the first to pass through the turnstiles. Not for me arriving with fifteen minutes to go. I wanted to see it all. I stood at the back with my husband, Paul, and watched the stadium fill up. It was a splendid sight and Hampden, with its dark green turf, and heightened atmosphere, was the most beautiful place in the world!

You either love Hampden or you hate it. I've always thought it a grand place - I like its solidity and the sense of history attached to it, I didn't mind that in places it needed a lick of paint or a facelift. And no matter how often United lost there I never feared its hoodoo or called for it to be razed to the ground. I had great misgivings about its refurbishment. I hate seating with every fibre of my being. It's not that I don't think that those fans who want to sit should be forced to stand for the rest of their lives, but I do believe that those of us who feel that seating is uncomfortable, restrictive and perhaps, dare I say it, dangerous, should be allowed house-room in every stadium. But you can't carry on a one-woman campaign forever against what seems to be a fait accompli, and reluctantly I have had to accept that standing at most football matches will soon be a thing of the past. I had to admit that Hampden, now wholly covered and with its full panoply of seats before me, was quite spectacular. Majestic and fitting for a National Stadium without being at all pretentious or ostentatious.

I looked at the goals and thought of all the great players who had scored there. Puskas, Di Stefano, Best, Muller, Charlton, Law, Greeves, Maradona, Dalglish, little knowing that Craig Brewster's name was about to be added to this roll of honour.

Looking upwards at the oval of sky, I watched the scudding clouds give way to clear blue, and the pitch became bathed in sunlight just as the fans arrived en masse. The noise and the atmosphere were quite overwhelming. The music, which is now so evocative, was very much part of the whole experience. United seemed to have all the best tunes. 'United, we're gonna win the Cup' – a repetitive and hypnotic chant – to 'Go West' by the Pet Shop Boys was sheer poetry to our ears! And then over the Tannoy came Deacon Blue's 'Dignity' and you couldn't hear yourself think for the sound of 12,000 voices accompanying Ricky Ross. Magic. And when they played Tina Turner's 'Simply the Best' we knew every word. A great sea of tangerine and black, swaying and singing in perfect harmony. No-one was sitting down and none of the stewards seemed to mind.

The Rangers' Appreciation Society seemed to be much less animated. They too could be seen singing and waving scarves and banners, but when you looked across at them it was not in unison. This was something of a conundrum at first. Why were they less vocal than we were? The answer may be a twofold one. Firstly, on close examination, you could see that many of the blue brigade had already taken their seats, and that the choristers were those who stood in pockets amongst them. The sedentary lifestyle at Ibrox has made them passive (ergo, seating is a negative influence in football. I rest my case). Moreover, there is no doubt that they would be more laid-back, more blasé, in their approach to this game. They had seen it all before. They had a look of superiority about them as if making a song and dance about something that was a virtual certainty was only for the likes of those who needed to boost their team's morale. After all, they supported the best team in the Universe.

Now, none of us were foolish enough to turn up thinking that United were the best team in the world, but we did feel that with a little help from their friends our team could do it. And on the day, the fans made all the difference.

The players arrived and walked out onto the pitch to survey the scene. Rangers first. Sober-suited. The Huns had arrived. Scottish football's master race. Huddled together in the centre circle in earnest debate. They wouldn't, of course, have been discussing the double-treble, they'd told everyone that that was the last thing on any of their minds. The thought of breaking records had never entered their heads. No, they would probably have been discussing environmental problems or the state of the economy, and wondering how they could find room in their already overflowing trophy room for one more piece of bric-a-brac. Suddenly Richard Gough broke free to inspect the surface. Funny how the patch of turf which merited his close attention happened to be near the cornerflag in front of the United support. Was that a complacent smirk playing on his lips?

Then United poured onto the pitch. A multicoloured ensemble with their different styles of dress. They were laughing and jumping about, reading programmes and responding to the row of the crowd. They marched straight past Walter Smith and his coterie of men and came to their fans. Rangers were inconsequential. And all the while Richard Gough and Co watched them, curious as to their relaxed demeanour and clearly discomfited by it.

The pre-match entertainment was, for want of a better word, naff. Whoever dreamt up the idea of a shooting competition to excite and engross the fans had plumbed the depths of mediocrity. Three representatives for United, and three for Rangers, stood in the centre circle and tried to score with a single long shot. I think United won, but I didn't care enough to keep a tally. At least the traditional appearance of a pipe band before the start of play renders some sense of occasion to the proceedings and provides some dignity. But the SFA, in its infinite wisdom, had decreed that such things were no longer fitting and that a 'cabaret' was more appropriate. At least the balloons were released and we watched as the sacks emptied and the sky swallowed up its offering.

And talking of balloons.... There was one golden moment when both sets of fans shouted as one. As Jim Farry, Chief Executive of the SFA, was introduced to the crowd everyone jeered. The SFA is not regarded by many as the friend of Scottish football, but its enemy. Park Gardens is not, it is believed, peopled by visionaries, but by loathsome bureaucrats and Lilliputians.

And the players took up their positions. Rangers in their very classy new true-blue strip. United in their one-off outfit, displaying, for the first time, the logo of their new sponsor - the car manufacturer - Rover.

How eagerly I then awaited the thing I had for so long dreaded. The start of play. United looked the part - a team of contrasts - light and shade. Inspired by youth and driven by experience. There was Malpas, Bowman and McInally - old timers - men of will and determination who were to drive and direct the whole operation; who dug their heels in and kept the team together. Dailly, McLaren and Hannah brought exuberance and tenacity, they showed no fear or deference. Petric and Welsh - complementary and contrasting. Petric so cool and calm, Welsh strong and decisive. Alex Cleland manning the barricades and sneaking forward to lend a hand up front. There was Brewster's threat at the front, the fastidiousness of Guido Van de Kamp at the back, and on the bench, steel and fire. And all of it held together by a little bit of Ivan Golac's magic. The perfect team selection and not one voice in the crowd was raised in protest. Had there been near me, I would have personally knee'd each dissenter in the groin!

And once the whistle signalled the start of play you became so utterly engrossed in it that nothing mattered beyond the confines of the pitch. You were excited and terrified at the same time. Time, you thought, would be bound to hang heavy but the amazing thing was that the game was over in the twinkling of an eye. It unfurled before us like an intricate tapestry, and just when you were admiring the patterns and the workmanship it was over. And all that you have left are your memories.

But what memories. What emotions.

Take for example, the heart-stopping moment, early on, when McPherson's header would have landed squarely in the net but for McInally who blocked it on the line. How many times in the past has McInally saved United's bacon with just such a clearance?

The sense of injustice when Alex Cleland sauntered into the penalty box only to be rugby tackled by Ian Ferguson. PENALTY - shouted the United crowd. NONSENSE said Dougie Hope, and play resumed.

And all the while McLaren, Dailly and Craig Brewster looked dangerous.

At half-time all the talk in the pie queues and the toilets was of how well United were playing. How, as time progressed, their belief in themselves grew. A goal, some said, was only round the corner. I found myself accosted by a man who started to reel off a long list of statistics relating to the game. Did I know how many times Maxwell had touched the ball? I did not. "Get a life" I thought. "Get a haircut" he suddenly shouted at Mark Hateley as the teams reappeared, and I warmed to him a little.

And then the goal. I remember it all so clearly. It is as if the slow motion, action replay cameras roll every time I think of it. I recall the look of horror on McPherson's face as he sent the ball back towards his keeper, a look which was matched only by the expression on Maxwell's. Here was a man who had been betrayed and mortally wounded by someone he knew and trusted, who, before you could say, "Oops" had fluffed the clearance from the ill-timed backpass. I remember Christian's composure as he picked up the ball and sent it across towards goal and the blur that was Craig Brewster as he raced in and thumped it into the net. WAHAY! The goal was no fluke. It had everything - farce, skill, suspense and ecstasy. I looked at Christian standing before us and I knew I loved him more than life itself. I loved Craig Brewster too. I even loved McPherson and Maxwell (and toyed briefly with the idea of calling this book KISSING RANGERS!). And then I panicked. Stricken. "Whatever was Brewster thinking of? It's only two minutes into the second-half and scoring against Rangers was tantamount to waving a red rag in front of a bull."

I wasn't the only one who went rigid with fear. All around me, amidst the dancing and the singing, there were fans staring straight in front of them, white and ghostly, fearing the worst. And we didn't have to wait long. Seven minutes to be precise when Alexei Mikhailitchenko picked up a McCall pass and turned and shot with such speed and velocity that it was unstoppable. Well, it might have been if Van de Kamp hadn't been in goal. How he got to it we'll never know, but I knew I had fallen in love again. The man beside me wanted to marry Guido and have his children.

By now I thought of escaping to the toilet, better still, of going home. But mesmerised by the spectacle and still believing that United could keep Rangers at bay I stood (yes, stood) rooted to the spot. Rangers advanced. United retreated. United advanced. Rangers retreated. Rangers, it seemed to me, did a lot of advancing and United a lot of retreating.

And all the while Mikhailitchenko, Durie and Hateley looked dangerous, but United's defence were more than a match for them and yielded nothing.

And just when you thought there was at least half an hour left on the clock Dougie Hope raised his Acme Thunderer to his lips and the shrill sound of the final whistle was drowned out by shouts of joy. It had been a graceful, gripping final United had not let us down, they had won the Cup and I was there. Me!

I could hardly believe it, but there before, and all around, me was the irrefutable evidence. The Rangers fans had disappeared, the United fans intoxicated with success, some temporarily with drink, were delirious, and the United players stood on the pitch, winners of the Scottish Cup and were cheered by every one of us. Cheers to cherish. A public moment, but also a very private one. Players and fans in communion. The party was just about to begin. I watched as each player in turn lifted the Cup and thought of those who had missed the chance to claim it. I looked at Alan Main, Billy McKinlay, Scott Crabbe and Paddy Connolly and I felt the tears well up in my eyes. I watched Paul Hegarty and David Narey and could hardly stop myself crying. But when the crowd called for Jim McLean I could control myself no longer and the tears ran down my cheeks.

Many thought that, after all these years of waiting, winning the Cup would be something of an anti-climax. Not for me, I found it awesome.

In the weeks and months that have passed nothing has tarnished the memory of that day. I have however, one quirk, one idiosyncrasy. Having set the timer on my video to capture every minute of the happy event, I have been unable to bring myself to watch it. I couldn't view the highlights on TV or buy the recently-produced video. I remember it as such a good match, and can't bear to watch it again just in case one minute of it turns out to be worse than I remembered. Maybe, in years to come, I will be able to sit down and relive that day - but for now, I'll get by on my memories.

# *Billy McKinlay*

Born in 1969 in Glasgow, Billy McKinlay joined United sixteen years later when still a schoolboy. A constructive and intelligent midfield schemer who is a master of ball control and precise passing. His shooting, as well as his sweeping crossfield passes, is also a valuable weapon for both club and country. Billy McKinlay has been involved in two of United's previous unsuccessful Cup finals. Sadly, this victory left him feeling much as though he'd lost another one.

---

# LOOK BACK IN ANGUISH

It was a highly debatable refereeing decision. It wasn't a bad tackle after all. Rob McKinnon just seemed to trip over Billy McKinlay's feet. And FIFA had yet to issue their post-World Cup instructions about clamping down on anything resembling physical contact during a match. Nonetheless the yellow card shown to McKinlay during the League match against Motherwell at Fir Park on 3rd May and the two points accompanying it were, to say the least, harsh and cruel considering the consequences for the player. Indeed, many believed that it could have had a detrimental effect on the outcome of the Cup final.

Billy McKinlay looks back on that moment and sighs. You can see it still hurts. The anguish is visible on his face. "Getting booked is inevitable given my style of play," he admits. Which isn't a confession that he's dirty or even hard. He plays with passion and commitment. "Even now," he says "I find myself thinking - if only I hadn't done this, or if only I had done that. I think of all the silly bookings I'd had over the season and think if only I had done things differently." Life is full of if onlys. It's the lament of all footballers and football fans. And yes, if only Referee McGilvray had counted to ten before reaching for his notebook he might well have had second thoughts and given the United player the traditional finger-wagging instead. It was all that the foul merited. And Billy McKinlay wouldn't have missed the Cup final.

It wasn't that Mr McGilvray wasn't aware of McKinlay's situation. It was common knowledge that an accumulation of points had placed him close to suspension. McKinlay himself had spoken to the referee before the game and assured him that he would do everything he could to avoid trouble. And it was clear to all who watched the match that McKinlay did indeed make strenuous efforts not to fall foul of the official. Furthermore, any hint that he was likely to booked and Ivan Golac would undoubtedly have protected him by taking him off.

Needless to say the yellow card was accompanied by a collective gasp of horror in the away quarter of the ground as it was realised that there we were, about to embark on the most important game of the season (of the last three seasons, in fact) without one of our players who was not only creative and influential but who had also contributed so much to the Cup run having played in all the preceding rounds. United's progression to the final owed much to McKinlay and for him to be denied the chance to play in it was a grave injustice. But if the fans were devastated just think how McKinlay himself must have felt. You only had to look at him to see how much of a personal tragedy this was. Overcome by angst and pain he wandered around the pitch in a daze for a few moments, the very picture of wretchedness and suffering, before being substituted. "I just couldn't have played on," he says, "I was absolutely destroyed. I held onto the hope for a few days that I'd only get one point against me for the foul and not two, which would have meant I would have avoided suspension, but really I was clutching at straws, but you'll clutch at anything when you're a drowning man."

So why then was McKinlay playing if there was any likelihood that he could miss the final? To tell the truth, United were in a spot of bother. The dreaded words 'relegation candidates' were being bandied about for the first time in almost twenty years. Panic was beginning to set in amongst those of little faith when a succession of poor results saw United uncomfortably near the bottom of the division. Victory at Motherwell who, it has to be remembered were having a particularly good season, would see off the scaremongers. It's always a case of all good men coming to the aid of the party, all hands to the pumps, when you're in mortal danger and Billy McKinlay and Jim McInally (who was in a similar predicament) were fielded. But was it a risk worth taking?

Opinions differ. Undoubtedly McKinlay is a class act. An exceptionally talented footballer who is greatly admired throughout the game, especially by those who are excited by skill and vision and courage. Billy McKinlay is he who dares. A match winner. A beautiful footballer. And when it's a case of character, conflict and competition you'll not find him wanting. Most managers would have made provisions to include him at some point during the match at Fir Park. With hindsight it was a decision which left the United fans more nervous about the Cup tie than they had been before the start of the Motherwell game (a game which, incidentally, United did win).

When Billy McKinlay reflects on the period leading up to the Cup final you get an insight into his despair. "It just keeps eating into you the whole time. You can't sleep, you can't think of anything else." While the other first team players were on a high, full of optimism and hope, it is clear that McKinlay felt isolated. There was no escape. "You must be sick at missing the final" were the words that greeted him at every turn. Even now, he wants to scream when someone repeats the phrase.

So what of Cup final day itself? "In actual fact, I thought I was going to cope quite well with it," he muses. "I'd enjoyed being away with the others in the days preceding the match. Even on the bus on the way to Hampden I amazed myself by managing to overcome my own feelings and become quite involved in the mood of optimism." But then that's Billy McKinlay. Life and soul of the party? So they say. Nothing gets him down? Maybe, but some things are just too powerful, too enormous to overcome. And anyway, there's much more to the player than the one-dimensional person we see on the park, he's a thoughtful, complex character who has a serious side to his nature.

"I was able to watch the game and become completely engrossed in it. I thought it was an exciting match and was genuinely delighted for the boys when they won." However when he walked onto the park he says the enormity of it all just hit him. "I felt like an alien." He was embarrassed and uncomfortable about being there. This was nothing to do with him and, no matter how often you tell him that this victory owed as much to the players who had played in the qualifying rounds as to those who turned out on the day, he can't accept it. If you suggest that his contribution merited a medal he simply says he wouldn't want one. He didn't even want a strip. And to this day he still can't handle it. The Cup that is. He can't bring himself to touch it. When you've channelled your whole career towards winning a trophy it becomes a symbol of all your pain. "I'm inclined to hide my head in the sand." he says, "When things upset me, I'd prefer not to confront them."

And as he wandered about the Hampden pitch, lost in a sea of laughing and joking, and later in the dressing-room when everyone was so full of joy, he knew there was only one thing he could do. He had to go home. "I couldn't hang around when everyone was on such a high. My face was tripping me and I didn't want to spoil it for the others. It was their day and I didn't want to be moping around with everyone feeling sorry for me." Neither does he want anyone to think it was a case of sour grapes or the spoiled brat type of petulance that made him give the celebrations a miss. It wasn't a case of self-pity or they-shouldn't-have-won-it-without-me attitude, it was simply an overwhelming feeling of alienation.

On thing he does remember with great pleasure. "The fans," he says, "were the best ever. They were brilliant and if half of those who went to other matches showed that much enthusiasm we'd win a lot more games."

And what, for Billy McKinlay will eradicate all the painful memories? Although it is likely always to be there in the back of his mind, he has plenty of distractions. His family for a start. As the father of three small children he won't have much time to dwell on his own woes. And playing helps too. "When you're on the pitch, your love of football takes over and you can forget past miseries." And then he becomes quite philosophical. "It had been such a good season for me sure as anything, something was bound to go wrong." And how!

McKinlay believes that this ghost will only finally be laid to rest for him when he is part of another United cup-winning side. And the sooner the better as far as he's concerned.

And so say all of us.

## Ricky Ross

To music fans and United supporters Ricky Ross needs little or no introduction. Until recently he was the lead singer and guiding light behind the internationally acclaimed band, Deacon Blue, which is now disbanded. His songs are widely regarded as classics and have a ring of familiarity and truth about them that make them both memorable and haunting. At the time of the Cup final his group's album was No 1 in the charts. He has long been a United fan and, like the lyrics of his songs, this story is a very personal one. Ricky Ross knows all about dignity.

# DIGNITY

MAY 1974

*United we stand divided we fall*
*And if our backs should ever be against the wall*
*we'll be together, together you and me.*

Blue Mink

We're walking out of Hampden, my dad and me, with my uncle and cousin. We've lost the Cup final to an all-conquering Celtic team that is favoured by my uncle. "No Spunk," my uncle reliably informs us, "that Dundee United team have no spunk!" My cousin and I snigger as we make our way to the car.

"At least we weren't humiliated," my dad consoles me. I take this on board until I return home to discover Celtic had put a third goal in when we were making our way out of the ground. Perhaps even that rude snigger would not have occurred to me then if I'd known how many of these end-of-season Saturdays I'd be leaving Hampden bitter and disappointed.

How Scots can love that place I'll never know. For me it's always been a desolate hole in the south side of Glasgow which swallows up ambition and destroys all dreams, compounding it all with the misery of its architecture, the disdain of its police officers and the general antipathy of Glaswegians to all footballing adventures beyond its city limits.

Hampden never read the script. It called me back again and again. Desolate afternoons witnessing Masonic referees all-but wearing a Rangers strip, dull, windy May days that threw the Hampden dirt up in our faces or grim, soaking Wednesday nights dutifully supporting a Scotland team whose management committee cared not a jot for the rain-sodden, long-suffering (stupid?) supporters. Oh yes, we've spent time at Hampden. All this time watching the grim old bowl, Samson-like, slowly being sapped of its one great strength – the fact that it was bigger and louder than any other stadium in Europe. Yes we were all drunk, hundreds of us passed out, we tripped lightly over vomit and urine and our sisterly supporters were allowed no toilet of their own but, God Dammit, we packed more in and ripped off more supporters than yer San Siro, Bernabeu and Parc des Princes put together!

So we came back again and again my old man and me. We witnessed the sudden conversion of Glaswegians from fervent Old Firm fans to St. Mirren supporters in 1987 – how we laughed – to their even more worrying free transfer to the colours of Motherwell in 1991. I was asked on the park for an opinion that day by the BBC who'd also invited two of the Steel Men's more noteworthy supporters to do the same thing. The only funny thing after that day was meeting a pal who said, "What were these two cunts from The River Detectives doing there? They're up at Parkhead every other Saturday." ... how we laughed.

MAY 1991

> *Lazarus wasn't grateful for his second wind*
> *another chance to watch his chances fade like the dawn ...*

> American Music Club

It's final number six and my father, now a south-side resident, has returned for the first time since 1974. We all go. My wife, my dad, my Celtic supporting, but ultimately football-starved, brother-in-law John, my best pals and companions of the previous four miseries, Warbeck and Linda. We blag some tickets off Dougie Donnelly for the reasons stated above and – to be honest – we're feeling good. We're better than them. They are not one of the 'big' teams and with a bit of luck we can out-sing them. We regularly go to Fir Park and would be disappointed to only draw. We have learned so much since 1987 against St. Mirren. 1988 we were always going to lose given that it was Celtic's centenary and the combined forces of the east end of Glasgow, the three remaining green fields of the Free State (and a fair chunk of the fourth) plus a massive amount of pressure on the Almighty by his Holiness the Pope didn't really give us a look in.

I even had the good fortune to bend one of the mighty ears of Paul Sturrock (no mean task) as the boys are warming up and he tells me the young lads don't care too much about the now legendary hoodoo and are looking forward to the match. What can go wrong?

Looking back now I find it ironic that these non-existent punters — the neutrals – were meant to have had a great day that day. We provided the neutrals with a great day! I would happily have taken responsibility for Dundee United putting large chunks of the western hemisphere *off* football if it had meant a dour midfield tussle and an own-goal to us somewhere along the line.

My dad walked out with much the same line as he'd given in 1974. He saved the worst for last however. As we sat there reeling from the shock and I began to wonder about the wisdom of bringing a not-entirely well man to such a heart-stopping event, Dad leaned over and opined that the following day the papers would only tell us that Motherwell deserved to win. How sadly true that turned out to be. The stars for merit in The Post and The Mail giving the final lie that they were better than us when the truth, as every true 'Arab' knew, was that there was a conspiracy that had been hatched by the CIA, MI6, The Orange Lodge, The Nights of St Columba, their umbrella organisation, The SFA, and the Dundee Courier that Dundee United wouldn't win the Scottish Cup. Motherwell paraded the cup in front of their 'supporters' … how we laughed.

1992-1993

> *Well I was young and didn't know what to do*
> *when I saw your best steps stolen away from you*
> *now I'll do what I can*
> *I'll walk like a man*
>
> Bruce Springsteen

A funny thing has happened to me. I've become a minor celebrity. I can get tickets to these big games that are always problematic as any Dundonian exile knows. I start to get posh tickets that are accompanied by half-time drinks and a pie or even a chat with the legendary Hamish McAlpine.

My Dad and I bump into Walter Smith and he invites us up to Ibrox for a meal before the United game. We have a great old time my dad and me and end up being shown round the trophy room by the considerate Walter. My dad reminds him that he's only doing this well because his assistant manager, first-team coach, captain, reserve coach and his good self are ex-

Tannadice boys. Walter takes all this on board and spends too much of his valuable time with a couple of away supporters whose main interest in him is not as manager of an unbeatable treble winning side but as the midfield work-horse whose boot-kissing celebration of a winning goal against Dundee adorned the opening credits of Sportscene for many a year.

We go up to Perth to see United play at the new McDiarmid Park. As I return from parking the car I find my father has managed to acquire three free tickets from Chairman, Jim McLean. I look behind me as we walk up the steep staircase to our seats. I'm appalled and embarrassed to see dad almost on all fours as he ascends the steps. I go down to help him and realise that the days of us going to the game together are numbered. He is not even fit enough for the modern stands that seem to be springing up all over the country. As we leave the ground it never occurs to me that we will not go to a game together again, far less that he will not see the end of the most memorable Dundee United season for eleven years.

My Dad and I had a great friendship that football, and particularly Dundee United, played a huge part in. We started going to games around 1968 and it was he who told me of the tradition that my grandfather had of going one week to see United and the other to see Dundee. A game a week. Something that Aberdonians could never enjoy and Glaswegians were too tribally entrenched to ever consider. He never came to the Wednesday night matches as it clashed with his habit of attending the prayer meetings at the church. This meant he was to miss out on some of the most memorable nights in the history of the club – a decision he wouldn't have changed even if he'd have known the result in advance. So we supported United against all-comers and cheered Dundee on – especially against Rangers and Celtic – and tried not to laugh if they were unexpectedly dumped by Clyde of an afternoon. (Bear in mind that the vast majority of Dundee people favoured Dundee FC in these days.) My part in all this was to queue for pies before, and after, half-time, if necessary, in return for being paid in and transported to the games. (A habit that was hard to break even until May 1994.)

We kept up this pattern of attendance until 1974 when the disillusion of the Cup final defeat, increased violence around football, and the unstoppable alienation that adolescence brings, drove our Saturday afternoons in separate ways. My dad took to the radio and I took to cruising record shops, part-time work and various other activities that partially distracted me from the main event. At the time of the 1991 semi-final against St. Johnstone I was in New York working and decided to phone my dad up for news on the game. He told me they were playing out the last five minutes and promptly stuck the phone by the radio while I listened, unable to do anything else. I realised that the radio was his Saturday afternoon companion, as once I had been, and felt no hurt at his choosing it over me when the call had come in.

I'd deserted our partnership all these years before and he wasn't going to let me break up a happy relationship again. The radio kept him involved in football and it was ironic that my father, the radio, and the fate of the Scottish Cup became fatally intertwined for me.

The call came about six-thirty on the Tuesday. I'd worn my strip into rehearsals that day and wound up everyone about the semi-final replay of that evening. I said we'd beat Aberdeen and then get stuffed by Killie in the final. We were at tea. I'd just got my daughter a yogurt from the fridge. I was anxious to hurry as I'd said I'd pop in on dad as I'd done on the Saturday to set up his walkman so he could tune in to the game. He was in the Victoria Infirmary near Hampden and it made sense to look in for ten minutes even though I'd seen him for proper visits over the weekend and would see him again tomorrow. I'd bought him some BBC tapes when I'd done a TV show at Pebble Mill the previous day and I wanted him to have them.

My wife answered. It was my mum sounding worried. She said the hospital had phoned to say that dad was going down fast and that I should come over quickly. By the time I arrived he'd passed away.

MAY 1994

> *And I'm thinking how good it would be*
> *to be here some day ...*

Deacon Blue

The reality is that I started to wish we'd get ingloriously dumped in the first round of any of a given year's competition. I hoped to enter the summer without the awful hangover of a final defeat. Here I was at Hampden having played our band's final concert the previous evening, been up all night drinking and talking and weeping on shoulders, rushing around Glasgow to get baby-sitting cover to suddenly walking into The Cup final to the sight and sound of the east end of the ground being bathed in tangerine and singing along to a song I had written. Even the night before, even dad's sudden death on the night of the semi-final replay, didn't prepare me for the emotion of that moment.

It went so quickly.

Years of habit taught me to go to the pie shop at half-time and not to return empty handed even if a cheer went up. Our wives were thirsty and wanted a drink of juice. Warbeck heard the teams come out and ran back to his seat. I remained glued to my post, the ghost of my dead father urging duty to the task; comforting me that one goal more missed in the service of a pie and a Bovril was as noble a sacrifice as a man could give. Even the cheer as Davy

McPherson idiotically passed the ball back didn't move me, the mighty shout as Christian Dailly hit the post only removed a couple of guys in front. It wasn't finally until Craig Brewster had hit the back of the net with, what turned out to be the winning goal, that I made my apologies to my father, forgot about the drinks and ran into the arms of Warbeck who had to tell me exactly what had happened as we danced on the Hampden seats. All I remember is that we finally discovered the guys behind us were closet Huns as my wife flicked her tangerine headgear accidentally into one of their faces in celebration – he wouldn't have minded if he'd been one of us.

At the end? I kissed Jim McInally on the mouth. I nearly got arrested for jumping onto the running track to hug Davie Bowman. I insisted on standing on the perimeter wall to see Maurice lift the cup even though a Hampden steward took great exception. I told him I'd been coming here for twenty years, that I wasn't going to miss this moment now and that there wouldn't be a court in the world who would find me guilty of a crime! As someone who'd spent the last few years coming to public occasions, if not wholly in disguise, then certainly dressed down, I then left Hampden and answered every person who called my name – not only admitting that I was in fact the big singer out of Deacon Blue – but hugging them and their children in a manner that would only be appropriate for reunited long-lost relatives. It was only then that we bought two flags which were ceremoniously hoisted through the sunroof of the car until a mixture of commonsense and police aggravation brought them inside.

As we drove through Langside we passed the Victoria Infirmary where my father had died just five weeks before; five weeks that had taken me round the country saying goodbye to thousands of people. My father had gone without so much as a wave from the stage and, after all our trips waiting and hoping, United had won the Scottish Cup without him even listening at home on the radio.

I suddenly realised that the first half of my life was over. After such a long wait it was finally over.

## POSTSCRIPT AUGUST 94

I'll go home soon. I'm writing this in my windowless dungeon in Kelvinside. It's a beautiful day outside and I'll phone up Warbeck tonight. We'll arrange to see each other, maybe a game of golf or a trip up to Dundee for the start of the season. When we get to a lull in the conversation one of us will say, "We won the Scottish Cup." "That's right," the other will reply, "We won the Scottish Cup."

# *Pat Ruddy*

Pat Ruddy was born in Dundee in 1967. He studied Electronics in Edinburgh and lived for three years in London, travelling up most weekends to watch United. He is currently running Brushed Nylon Theatre Company in Edinburgh.

---

# A BEAUTIFUL LIFE

Life should be lived with confidence and optimism, lust and passion, arrogance and self-belief and, above all, love. Where any one of these factors is lacking a gap appears and we cannot continue on an even keel. The same can be said for football fanaticism. The fan who constantly decries his team, criticises players and calls for the manager's head cannot, in all honesty, share completely in the spoils at the end of the season. He has alienated himself from victory whilst attempting to disassociate himself from defeat. For this hollow fan there is the nagging guilt that he did not give his all through the season. He does not deserve to be an integral part of the final celebration. This, at first, may seem harsh but by denying his team he has foregone his right to the rewards.

What causes these people to lose faith in the team? What is the force which turns them away from the men they worship? In my opinion, it is the loss of courage. The fear of allying themselves with failure and the inability to take a small portion of the blame for that failure. A football game hinges on more than twenty-eight players and two managers - the fans play an enormous role in the proceedings and consequently, if the team loses, the fans must share the blame for the defeat and it is the failure to accept this fact which creates the kind of negative haranguing that we have heard from the stands and the terracing over the last few seasons.

If any of you have shouted negative things at a young player like Christian Dailly, hang your head in shame. If you are part of the contingent who called for Golac's resignation at Pittodrie, understand the depths of your ignorance. You know who you are and you must live with your guilt. I know that I would find it very difficult. You must line yourselves up with the ex-Dundee fans who creep into Tannadice to watch the better team saying, "I've aye supported United". This is the cross you must bear. Perhaps I'm misguided but I wouldn't piss in your ear if you head was on fire.

The 1993/94 season has been one in which the qualities of arrogance and self-confidence have begun to shine through again at Tannadice for the first time in the 90's. This is mainly due to the managerial appointment of the flamboyant Ivan Golac who, despite being seen as a green newcomer with misplaced overoptimism, is a tactical giant. His interview style keeps the press in his pocket and provides unrivalled entertainment for the true fan. Not for us the "we'll take each game as it comes" or "the boys done good", but as if from the quill of Byron or Browning, or the works of Albert Camus, we have, "if you can't understand nature, you can't understand football." Win or lose we can all count on top quality entertainment from the manager.

The confidence brought by Ivan Golac has rubbed off on a contingent of the travelling support and has produced results which make the away terraces buzz with atmosphere. This small hardcore of fans must be congratulated on their wonderful array of new songs and undying optimism throughout the season. Who could fail to enjoy the chants of 'One shoe, you've only got one shoe' at Ibrox last season? Who could deny that the production of a hundred or so A4 sheets with 3 - 0 printed on them in large letters, was the funniest sight at any Scottish football ground in the last year (although it has to be said that Sieb Dykstra's frustrated gestures to the crowd after his double blunder during our last visit to Fir Park came a close second)? If only this party atmosphere which we take with us around the country could be reproduced at Tannadice then I'm certain that we could be in contention for greater honours in the seasons to come.

So, no thanks to all the moaners, we won the Scottish Cup last season for the first time in our history. A campaign which spanned nine games and employed eighteen players on the way to one of the greatest moments in United's history. We began rather ignominiously at Gayfield when the wind, rain and a determined Arbroath side (marshalled brilliantly by ex-United bicycle-kick hero, Charlie Adam) all conspired to bring us down. What must Gordan Petric think, after playing in front of 80,000 in Belgrade in a top class stadium, having to come to a muddy field surrounded by a couple of sheds with people pissing behind them? From that lowly beginning we went on to face Airdrie (twice), Motherwell (twice), Aberdeen (twice) then finally - Rangers. It was no small achievement - in winning the Cup United beat the top three sides in the Premier Division - and we didn't lose at Hampden.

The only thing which struck at the hearts of all sensitive supporters was the dreadful state of the away strip. It amazed me to see the popularity of this dismal piece of leisurewear amongst the fans. It was downright embarrassing to see your team run out at Motherwell, Hearts, Aberdeen and Partick to the jeers of the home fans. I felt that the club had let themselves down by agreeing to appear in a sub-standard Jackson Pollock imitation costume. The thing was - and I don't want to become overly superstitious here - we did outrageously well whilst wearing that terrible smock. We didn't lose at Hampden in the semi-final in it. Maybe the opponents were too busy being doubled up with laughter to play to their best ability. I don't know. The good news is that this season heralds a return to sanity and has produced one of the finest strips ever seen for the away kit.

The day of the final is something of a haze for me. You want to savour every moment of it, be there with friends and make the most of it, but still my memories are hazy. It was just all so overwhelming. Fifteen of us agreed to meet in Glasgow and although you're in good company, having a few drinks, all the while you're trying not to think about the game itself. This was United's best chance of winning the Cup. It had to be Rangers they played. If it had been the other semi-finalists, Kilmarnock, the team just wouldn't have had quite the same motivation. Yes, it had to be Rangers.

You get a taxi to the ground and you're there and suddenly it's kick-off. And no matter how often you think about what it's going to be like when you win the Scottish Cup you can never imagine the feeling when you do. You go through every emotion - I remember that when the goal was scored I felt stunned. I couldn't believe it had happened - the ball had actually gone in the net - and I looked round me and while there were people going berserk with joy there were also quite a few who were ashen-faced, more than one of our group looked ill.

The goal itself brought a special sort of warmth to my heart. When I was a boy of ten and at school, the Primary Sevens played competitive football with the other school teams in the city, whilst the Primary Sixes had to go swimming. In mid-November 1978 I discovered that somehow, despite the stringent hygiene guidelines laid down by the Council's Recreation Department, I had contracted a verruca. This kept me off the swimming for some weeks. So on a Wednesday afternoon, instead of trotting off to the leisure centre with my towel roll and shivery bite, I went along with the headmaster to watch the older boys play football.

The team of 1978 was one of the best teams that Muirhead Primary School ever had. Their captain, although not very big, had the skill and arrogance which betrayed a great future in the game. They had another Dundee select player - Steve McIntyre - who was hard, fast and skillful, and Rab McLean was pretty good too. I was in awe of these players. I would be struggling to get a position on the bench the next season so these boys were like heroes to me and I watched wide-eyed as they dazzled with their silky one-touch football in those weeks that I nursed my verruca.

The last game that I saw that team play before my affliction disappeared and I was sent back to the baths was, if my memory serves me correctly, against Charleston at Birkhill Park. I watched my dream team troop out, resplendent in their thick red clinging nylon shirts and black shorts. I was carrying the kit-bag and I stood on the touchline for the whole of the first-half, my eyes glued to the spectacle in front of me. At half-time, when the players came off the field for their oranges, Muirhead were 13 - 0 up. Just before the restart the headmaster, Mr Fimister, came up to me and said "Get stripped, you're going on". To put in perspective how outrageous this suggestion was I must explain that at the age of ten I was still wearing age six trousers and was a good foot, foot and a half, shorter than the smallest players on the field, but he didn't have to repeat his offer. I quickly drowned myself in one of the spare strips and waddled out into a midfield position. To be honest, I didn't make much impression on the game. I was just back after injury, after all, but I joined in the celebrations as the team increased their lead to fifteen goals. About fifteen minutes before the end we got a penalty. The captain placed the ball on the spot, turned round and said, "Patty, Patty, come on up. You're taking it." Me? Me? Jesus! So I gathered my flapping strip round me and somehow in my daze I thumped the ball to the left of the keeper between the unnetted posts. I will never forget that moment until the day I die. If that had been the end of the story I would always owe a debt of gratitude to the captain. He had given me one of the things that make childhood worthwhile. So when I saw the captain score the winning goal in the 1994 Scottish Cup final I knew that my hero was, and always would be, the almighty Craig Brewster.

Wouldn't it be a lovely thought if we managed to hold on to half the United away support who attended the final? Even a quarter would do. I know that it is a vain hope and that we'll be back to the small hardcore when we travel to the likes of Kilmarnock next year, but it would be nice to think that winning the Scottish Cup would encourage a few armchair thumpers to cast off their indifference and become enslaved by the beautiful tangerine game. It is an enslavement - there is no doubt about that. Once hooked you can never get away from it. You'll try flirting with DIY and gardening but in the end there's no substitute for a 3 - 0 victory at Ibrox and you know it.

So what is the solution for the would-be total fan? In my opinion a fan should come to a game to enjoy it, to cheer for the team, and to bask in the occasional beauty which is created on the field. The fan is integral to the game. Therefore the fan has to take part of the responsibility for defeat. If we lose 5 - 0 then you didn't cheer loudly enough. It's as simple as that. It's just not good enough just to turn up, you must turn up with hope, with confidence and with unshirking love.

## *Peter Rundo*

In the early Sixties Peter Rundo could be seen outside Tannadice with an armful of United's programmes, and now he's programme seller turned, well, programme seller extraordinaire - but at the ripe old age of 46 he feels he's a little too long in the tooth to stand about on street corners plying his wares. Now he sells programmes to collectors as well as to the ordinary fan. He also writes and edits United's programme - amongst others. So you see, football programmes of all shapes and sizes are his livelihood - he claims to have the best collection of Dundee United programmes in existance. Married to Cath he is, first and foremost, a United supporter and has seen every game, with the exception of one, since Maurice Malpas made his debut. It was one of his greatest ambitions to see the United Captain lift the Scottish Cup - an ambition he has yet to fulfill...

---

# WHEN MO WENT UP TO LIFT THE SCOTTISH CUP....

On my first visit to Tannadice I saw something which has never been repeated - a Dundee United player - making his debut - scored a hat-trick. The player in question was Tommy Campbell. What I didn't realise then was that one of the opposition players that day would end up as United's chairman - he was, of course, none other than Jim McLean.

Prior to that visit I had watched Dundee, mainly because everyone else I knew supported the Dens Park side and I just tagged along. When I reached the age of reason I decided that the time had come to be different. In fact when I started secondary school I think that apart from Christian Dailly's father, Dan, I was the only United supporter in the class. With hindsight I feel that mine was a wise choice.

Success was to come quickly. Within eight weeks they were promoted, although not as Second Division champions, and really the club hasn't looked back since. Success is relative, and for United just being in the First Division was success enough. If thirty years ago anyone had suggested any of the names now associated with United's role of honour, not to mention the revamped stadium, they would have been met with total derision. Such things were Dundee's domain and not associated with the upstarts from Tannadice. Now the roles are somewhat reversed. And that's why so many of the older Dundee supporters are very bitter about United's success. And winning the Scottish Cup, the one claim to fame that our neighbours could gloat about in our hearing, is now thankfully missing from their armoury.

Having suffered through six Cup final defeats, the thought of a seventh was too much to contemplate, consequently I had worked myself into a fit of depression prior to the game and so, no matter how bad it turned out to be, any kind of victory was going to be fantastic. Quite frankly I didn't care how United won.

Undertaking my task to update information on the Tannadice Hotline meant that I was to have a bird's eye view from the perilously perched press box - with few United supporters around me - Jim Spence from BBC Radio Scotland being my one compatriot in the sky - but there was scant opportunity for little more than intermittent communication with him during the game.

I confess that my depression was beginning to lift as half-time approached. The team's performance was very encouraging. I hate to say I told you so, but I did say to a journalist sitting next to me that Maxwell, the Rangers' goalkeeper, looked as though he was struggling every time he was put under pressure at back-passes. And lo and behold, two minutes later, two former Harris Academy pupils (my old school) combined to rid United of the Cup hoodoo. Unfortunately there was another 40-odd minutes to endure and what had happened against Celtic on two previous occasions was all too readily recalled. In this instance, and remember United had never beaten Rangers in any Cup tie, forty minutes seemed like an eternity. Mercifully Rangers only really threatened to score on one occasion when Mikhailitchenko hit a shot on the turn which Guido Van de Kamp tipped over the bar. I think that it was at this point that I instinctively felt that this was going to be our day. Nonetheless it didn't seem to help time pass more quickly. I was so tense that I seemed to be looking at my watch every thirty seconds or so. And I suddenly remembered that I had a report to do and although I had taken copious notes they were hard to decipher.

My first thought was to sing "We won the Cup" down the line, but since I can't sing for toffee I quickly cobbled together a quick resume of the match which I rang in and left for those who were to call the Hotline, not surprisingly there were a lot more callers than usual!

As soon as the game was over I raced to meet my wife and a friend who had been in another part of the ground - bumping into Craig Brown, the

Scotland boss, on the way - and then took the fastest road back home to Gauldry for a quick pint.

When I sat back to analyse my emotions I realised that the most overwhelming one was relief. We had actually won, and in a way it was perhaps better than winning the Championship in the 1982/83 season for we had suffered so much in pursuit of this trophy. We had finally managed to rid ourselves of the stigma attached to being Cup final runners-up on so many occasions. It is extremely difficult to adequately express what such a victory meant to me and other United fans - only those of us who have been through the pain of past defeats can fully appreciate the emotional impact associated with winning the Scottish Cup.

And even though I hadn't cared how United won the game the great joy for everyone was that few could deny the fact that they actually deserved to win and the game had not been disappointing.

I was fortunate enough to be invited to join the team in the celebrations in the Earl Grey Hotel in Dundee that night. Undoubtedly it is every supporter's dream to celebrate success, particularly such sweet success, with the men who made it possible. They tell me it was a great night and I had a wonderful time!

My one regret was that when the final whistle blew and Maurice Malpas went up to lift the Scottish Cup I didn't see it. I simply didn't fancy bungie jumping out of the press box to gaze upon the scene below.

## *Matthew Watson*

Aged ten, Matthew has been going to watch Dundee United since he was six. He attends Edzell Primary School and plays for the school football team. This is not Matthew's first attempt to put his thoughts on paper – he has already written a book about Billy McKinlay (his favourite player) which, as yet, is unpublished; he often corresponds with the players and the manager giving them tips and advice for games. This is Matthew's story.

# WITH ALL OUR HEARTS

My Grandad is a United supporter and he used to be a Baptist minister before he retired. He knows a lot of stuff about the Bible and he told me about this verse in Colossians 3 verse 23:

*WHATEVER YOU DO, WORK AT IT WITH ALL YOUR HEART*

As well as going to the matches on Saturdays, it is my hobby to write to Mr Golac and Mr McLean and the players, and sometimes I get a cheery reply. My preparations for the final started after the semi when I was thinking about what I would write to the players. I began with some help from Grandad. If we worked at it with all our hearts, we would win.

As a supporter I like to think that I am helping the club, although I can't play for them until I'm older, and I haven't got much money. Dad says we can all contribute something, so I write to tell them my ideas and what I think.

We suffered more than most for the final. Dad had never driven to, or in, Glasgow before, so we arranged to go down on Friday afternoon when the roads were quiet and stay overnight with friends, Mr and Mrs Davidson, who are Rangers' supporters. Tom, Elizabeth and Maggie made us very welcome and we chatted about the game. Elizabeth was very concerned in case we got mugged travelling across Glasgow in our colours, so she lent us a backpack to put them in.

I stayed up late, till after 10.00pm. Dad said, "Don't tell Mum" and I wondered what the players were doing.

I got up at 9.00am and had a Billy McKinlay breakfast – cereal and a banana (usually I have Frosties). Billy is my favourite player and he told me that this was his usual matchday breakfast in a questionnaire I made up and he filled in for me. I usually have a Billy McKinlay breakfast before a match when I'm playing too. Dad read the previews of the match in the papers while I watched television and then we had a game of snooker. The Davidsons are 'true blues' and the only green things I saw in their house were a few plants and the snooker table! Dad won. I thought the players would be relaxing in the morning and I wondered what they would be having for lunch. Elizabeth made us cheeseburgers for lunch about 12.30pm - I hoped they weren't 'John Greig Burgers'. Then it was time to get ready to go.

Dad and I had bought orange mop-top wigs and when we appeared in them everyone laughed. Elizabeth said that we should put them in the backpack. This we did and then we set off – Tom, Maggie, me, dad and another Rangers' supporter called Gordon. It didn't take us long to get to the ground and when we parked we wished each other good luck and set off for our different ends. Gordon didn't speak much - he was a bit grumpy, but not as miserable as he was going to be! I wondered if all Rangers' fans were so unfriendly.

We walked through the park to get to the ground and there were a lot of Rangers' supporters around, drinking beer. They all seemed to be looking at us. We saw a few other United fans and they had kids with them. I kept close to my Dad and I felt better when we got to our end - Section F.

We had to have the backpack searched by a policeman before we got into the ground. We found our seats and I was glad when I realised that we were going to have a good view.

They have some lady stewards at Hampden and the one on our passage was really nice. Dad says I should write to Jim McLean and advise him to get some at Tannadice!

We opened the programme and Priti Trivedi, who is United's secretary, is much nicer looking than the Rangers' secretary. The programme looks a good buy for £2 - I'll read it properly later.

Our end of the ground seemed to be filling up quicker than the Rangers' end. Some people were putting up their banners. We were keeping ours until half-time, but we put our scarves and wigs on and as we did the players came out. We were all singing. I especially liked 'United, we're gonna win the Cup' (to the Pet Shop Boys' 'Go West'), and Tina Turner's 'Simply the Best'.

We waved and cheered and the players seemed pleased to see us.

Oh no, it looks like United are wearing the home strip and we're wearing our away strips. I wish I had known what strip United were going to wear, I hope that being in the wrong strip isn't going to be unlucky. The players weren't able to do their usual warm-up because of the shooting competition. I hoped that wasn't going to be a problem so we gave them another burst of 'We're gonna win the Cup'. They disappeared, but it didn't seem long before they were back and lined up for the off.

I hope that they got the messages I had sent:

'Guido, you'll do fine. I just know everything will stick to your gloves today.'

'Alex, I fancy a goal from an unusual source today.' (And we nearly got one.)

'Brian, if you get a chance to go upfield, go up the middle. Rangers will fade away in front of you.'

'Gordan, Mr Ice, play well and we'll build a win around you.'

'Capitaino, keep the young guns' heads up and play for 90 minutes.'

'David B, this is your day, drive United forward, make them play and be an encourager.'

'Jim, this is the Jim McInally final. Pour all over them.'

'Christian, run at them from deep and our young players will win this final for us.'

'Andy, be cool like Cantona and explode like Giggs.'

'Craig, shoot on sight. Rangers will back off if you run at them.'

'Jerren, relax, don't let them intimidate you.'

3.15. We're playing well. Guido dropped one of his first touches, but the ref had given a foul against McCoist. Nice one Jim - off the line. Brian hasn't lost anything important against Hateley. Should have been a penalty, but this is Glasgow. Christian is moving well. Craig looks like he means business.

3.30. The game is flying by, it'll soon be half-time. We're doing OK. Rangers aren't showing much - all the good stuff is coming from us. The defence is solid. Jim and Dave B are in charge in the middle of the park

Craig, Andy and Christian have a goal coming from one of them. Any one will do.

3.45 Half-time already. Forty-five minutes just disappeared. I wonder what they're saying in the dressingroom. Just get a goal in the second-half and we'll win this. We're really going to do it this time. The burgers and the drinks are better than ours (and a bit more expensive). Bigger is better when you're ten years old. I must write to Mr McLean about that.

Wait till you see our banner, bluenose. I can see one nearby with UNITED SCOTTISH CUP 74,81,85,87,88, 91 and 94 crossed out. Ours says, THIS IS THE DAY - UNITED - SCOTTISH CUP 94 - 21ST MAY. Magic. It's spread over four rows. I wonder if I'll be allowed to fly it at Tannadice. What do you think of that, Rangers? We're gonna win the Cup! THIS IS THE DAY. I wonder if I'll see our banner on TV.

The players are out again, here we go. What's this? WHAT'S THIS? Come on Christian - the post, BREWS..... GOAL!! OH YES!! UNITED!! YES.

The man next to me is slumped in his seat, head in his hands. Dad is muttering something about too soon, too soon. How long to go? Forty minutes.

I wrote to Andy McL after the semi, when he nearly got on top of one of Snelders' kick-outs, and told him that Maxwell was dodgy at kick-outs. I wonder if he remembered, maybe he told Christian.

And I claim an 'assist' for Craig's goal against Motherwell that helped save us from relegation because I knew that Dykstra sometimes didn't take the ball cleanly and we would get something if we followed up on our shots. And now Craig's done it again in the final. Hey Dad..... Jim, Ivan, Walter Smith - I practically scored our goal!! This IS the day!!

4.15. Rangers are pushing us a bit now, but we aren't in any serious trouble. Brian's still got Hateley under wraps. McCoist's done nothing. And we're still in control in midfield. David H is playing out of his skin - he's everywhere, I hope he doesn't get caught out of position. Tighten up on McCall and McPherson and we'll get there, and be careful of the Russian guy.

4.30. The second-half, like the first, is just flying by. McPherson is pushing up. Come on United, surely we aren't going to lose a goal to that big duffer. We aren't going to lose now, just don't defend so far back. Our attack isn't quite so fluid now. Come on the old heads - Jim, Dave B, Maurice - push up now, just one more time and we could get another goal and seal it.

Four minutes to go. Everyone is whistling. So is the ref. It's over, we've won. OH YES. UNITED! I can see the players grinning at us from here. Hey Craig. Hey Bo. Hey Jerren. Hey Ivan. WE WON!!

There goes Maurice. He's got it. He's got it. We've won the Scottish Cup.

We stayed and cheered all the players and sang, even though we had no voices left. 'YOU'LL NEVER WALK ALONE'. Magic. Then we went round to the main entrance to see the players getting on the bus. We passed a woman who had an orange T-shirt with something about Ivan's Hungry Boys on it and she was saying it must have been her T-shirt that did it. Yeah - and our wigs and the THIS IS THE DAY banner.

There were about three hundred United fans waiting to see the players off with the Cup. We cheered each of them and some of them clapped us. We met up with Tom and Kevin who sit behind us at Tannadice and they were hoarse too. They liked our wigs. We booed the Rangers' players and they looked miserable. About twenty of their fans had stayed to cheer them. I don't think the Rangers' players are very sporting, only McCoist smiled and waved when we sang 'Where's Your Treble Gone?' to the Chirpy, Chirpy, Cheep, Cheep tune. It was really funny. I saw Alan Main, he was smiling, but his eyes were sad. Never mind, Alan - next year. We would have liked to have seen Jim McLean with the Cup. Maybe later.

And as we left Hampden we passed a Rangers' supporters' bus from Dumfries and they gave us the thumbs up, shook hands with us and said well done, and that was nice. I was a bit worried about getting home, but the Rangers' support had all gone. They had left a lot of bottles and cans behind. I thought it can't be very nice to live around here when people leave all this mess.

We got on the train with some other United fans and chatted on the way into town. A lady and a gentleman from Arran said that they had waited fifty years for this day. Another man said he thought it was diabolical that Rangers had brought on Duncan Ferguson in the circumstances. Most of us didn't care - we'd got a new stand, Craig, Jerren, Gordan Petric and the Scottish Cup.

We all agreed that we would have liked to have seen auld Jim with the Cup, and the man from Arran said that Jim McLean had shown them round Tannadice and that he was a real gentleman, and we all agreed with him.

When we got back to the Davidsons they were very kind, considering they had been well-beaten. We chatted about the match and had a cup of tea and then Dad felt ready to drive home. We said our thank-yous and our good-byes and set off. The roads were quiet and when we got out of Glasgow we flew the scarf out of the window. We passed several other cars flying colours and one bus waved and cheered when we went past. Not you, Dad, keep your hands on the wheel!!

At the Invergowrie roundabout there was a WELL DONE DUFC banner, I hope the players see it and appreciate how much work kids put into making banners.

We got home in time to see the highlights on television and told Mum all about it. Then it was time for bed and I just thought, 'Yeah - we did it, we worked hard for it and we did it'. When Grandad gets back from his holiday I'll be able to tell him that the day we won the Scottish Cup we did it with all our hearts.

# *Mike Watson*

Mike Watson is the Member of Parliament for Glasgow Central. He was the author of RAGS TO RICHES: THE OFFICIAL HISTORY OF DUNDEE UNITED, published in 1985 and updated in 1992. He is a regular contributor to the United fanzine THE FINAL HURDLE, now happily renamed THE FINAL HURDL'D!

---

# THE BEST OF DAYS

It was the best of days, it was the worst of days.

It was, in fact, 12th April, and United were due to face Aberdeen in the Scottish Cup semi-final replay. It was the worst of days because it was a Tuesday and I had to be 400 miles away in London, my hold on events so tenuous it was restricted to following the match on Ceefax, returning every ten minutes for a 'fix'. When eventually it showed that Jim McInally's golden boot had fired the Terrors into the lead, my heart raced and my eyes glazed over, trained on the motionless screen, desperately hoping it would remain that way.

Alternatively I could have phoned my wife and asked her to hold the BBC Radio Scotland live commentary to the mouthpiece. Instead I sought sanctuary in the Chamber of the House of Commons for the remaining fifteen minutes, shutting out the real world, Hampden Park and everything else. What the House was debating I have no more idea now than I had at the time, but it offered respite for my fraying nerves.

Needless to say, it merely delayed the inevitable - I had to worship once more at the Ceefax altar, praying for confirmation that the final whistle had sounded on a famous victory.

Only the fact that the television which I consulted was to be found amidst the inviolable serenity of the House of Commons library prevented me from letting out a triumphant shriek on discovering that the scoreline had not altered and United were once more in the Scottish Cup final. The best of days. Only then did I begin to relive the nightmares of six previous finals, each one indelibly etched on my heart and once again my stomach began to churn. The worst of days.

Twenty-four hours later, it was confirmed that our Hampden opponents were to be Rangers, winners of everything except Wimbledon (mixed doubles) and the Eurovision Song Contest over the past three years, and in search of a final triumph to secure an unprecedented second consecutive domestic treble. Big deal. United hadn't won a thing for eleven years, so who was under more pressure?

At that time the final seemed a long way off, and indeed it was: five and a half weeks to be precise. Plenty of time for me to recall, and implement, the pledge I made after the fiasco of the 1991 final. I like to think that I'm a fairly mild-mannered sort of guy but the thing most likely to provoke me to physical assault is to be reminded that United's 4 - 3 extra-time defeat by Motherwell, on that occasion, was an enthralling match; one of the best finals ever; superb entertainment. Tell that to any Arab - then stand well back.

Trudging home after that dreadful experience - living a mere twenty minute walk from our National Stadium, tradition has seen me slamming my front door before United's opponents have completed their lap of honour - I swore that defeat number six was the limit, and I could take no more. I would spare myself further torture by staying away from future Scottish Cup finals until United had beaten what was, without a shadow of doubt, a hideous Hampden hoodoo.

In the three years which followed, the strength of my conviction had hardly been tested - not even a quarter-final place had been achieved. But here we were, in the first year of the reign of King Ivan, once again part of the blue riband of the Scottish season. So what should I do? My resolve held for the first week or so. "I won't be there." I brazenly announced to anyone willing to listen. "I'll spend the week-end in London." For the first two weeks, rather like the comment from the man jumping from a multi-story building as he passed the fifteenth floor, it was a case of 'no problems so far'.

Then the tickets went on sale and I began to waver. Neil Glen and Ian Allan, my neighbours in the spanking new George Fox stand at Tannadice, suggested buying a group of seats together for ourselves and friends. Alright, I thought, if I do change my mind and decide to go at the last minute, I can hardly do so if I don't have a ticket, can I?

In retrospect, it is clear that by this time my resolve was well and truly crumbling - although I maintained at least a facade of defiance during the weeks approaching the final, clearly convincing no-one in the process.

If I had to identify a single reason why I began to melt in the face of what everyone in Scottish football, except Arabs, predicted was certain to be gubbing number seven for United, I would utter but two words: Ivan Golac.

That feeling was more instinct than anything else - it certainly couldn't have been founded on logic, because we Arabs were witnessing, with reality suspended, the completion of United's worst League season for eighteen years. Jangling nerves were barely quelled by a finish which saw us avoid the jaws of the relegation zone by a mere two points. A Cup final boost it was not!

And then there was Rangers, by some distance the best team in Scotland - although with their resources they bloody well ought to be. But invincible? Certainly not. United had inflicted their heaviest defeat of the season with that comprehensive 3 - 0 win at Ibrox in December, so Golac and his players knew what was possible if Rangers were below their best.

Having said that, it would be wrong to give the impression that I was confident as the final approached. Not just about the outcome, but that I would be in my place to witness it. With previous finals I had enjoyed the build-up, voraciously devouring every word written about it and, in the week before the match, buying three or four newspapers each day. Not this time. In fact I studiously avoided the back pages to such an extent that had Guido Van de Kamp broken an arm, or Craig Brewster a leg, I would scarcely have been aware of it.

Of course, any such development would have been to pile disaster on top of tragedy, following the loss for the final of Billy McKinlay through suspension. Had the securing of a least a point from the third last League match not been essential, then McKinlay would not have played against Motherwell on 3rd May. 'Badger' has shown outstanding form, both in inspirational and goal-scoring terms, throughout the season, and had been justly rewarded with a place in the full Scotland team. So he was needed that night as United found themselves in the ignominious position where relegation remained a mathematical possibility.

He played a typical part, creating both of United's goals in their 2 -1 win at Fir Park, but at a heavy price; a yellow card for a relatively innocuous tackle lifted him over the limit on points and out of the final. I will long remember the look on Billy's face as the consequences of the referee's card-waving dawned on him. His absence devalued the final and was a cruel blow to a superb young player who, along with his colleagues, had battled through seven Scottish Cup ties for the right to perform on the stage which is the pinnacle of their careers for most players. The disciplinary points system is necessary but surely Cup finals should be excluded from such punishments. Either that, or points collected in League matches should apply only to that competition, and the same with the Cups. (Would I have felt as cheated had the victim been, say, Mark Hateley? Probably not.)

So United would have one further obstacle to surmount on 21st May while the media had yet more ammunition to fire in its 'Rangers can't lose' offensive.

Meanwhile my unprecedented low-key approach to the final was continuing, with the match being held at arm's length, right down to the day before. That changed significantly when I chanced upon BBC Scotland's preview that evening. It focused on both teams, and Hazel Irvine had been dispatched to United's hotel where she was making her usual ham-fisted attempt at interviewing Ivan Golac and several of his players.

Before my political correctness is questioned, let me say that I am delighted to see women breaking into the previously all-male world of football and, indeed, other sports. It represents a welcome breath of fresh air, but Hazel has the same effect on me as chalk scratching a blackboard, second only to the sugary-smug, Dougie Donnelly. Sportscene (or Scotsport) should make a bold entry into the transfer market and rescue Lorraine Kelly from Breakfast TV with an offer she can't refuse. And not just because she's an Arab; she actually understands the game and might ask informed, even searching, questions of the players, an art apparently alien to our Hazel.

But I digress. What I found surprising, though at the same time inspiring, was the confidence self-evidently abroad in the United camp. This was not the United of old, the cautious, tentative, hope-to-do-well approach of the McLean era. That Friday afternoon had been spent at Hamilton races and the players interviewed, like the manager himself, came across as both relaxed and self-assured. I seemed to absorb their optimism, developing from a feeling that Golac could lead the team to a historic win, to a belief that he would do just that.

Wise after the event, or a confident fig-leaf for the abandonment of my fighting words after the semi-final? Whatever, I had to be there.

And so to the great day. As evidence that I really had not made up my mind in advance to be there, I had not followed my practice for the 1991 final of getting local councillors to free me for the pre-match 'preparations' by covering my Saturday morning advice surgeries. So for two hours I dealt with constituents' housing complaints, immigration appeals, benefits claims plus the obligatory petition against the transport of live animals.

By the time I had finished, returned home, changed and met up with the travelling Arabs, it was gone one o'clock. We are a superstitious bunch, so the pre-final watering hole just had to be the same one used before (and after, naturally) the semi-final, and replay, against Aberdeen. Frixo's happens to be my local and was thus well-filled with familiar faces, quite apart from those down from the North East. Not surprisingly, after all the bravado about staying away from the final, my presence meant I was forced to consume enough humble pie to induce a sharp attack of indigestion, though two or three large Budweisers acted as sufficient chasers.

All good fun, but the festive air at Frixo's, which included some boisterous, though good-natured, banter with those sporting red, white and blue, was lost as we began the trek to Hampden. The out-of-town Rangers buses were disgorging their hordes, many of whom unashamedly relieved themselves without even the courtesy of entering a close. I wondered with what reproach a constituent might issue me, were he or she to witness these events, while their Member of Parliament strolled along apparently oblivious.

But such minor concerns were quickly overtaken by more serious ones. Our meeting place was to the west of Hampden, with the result that there were few tangerine and black scarves and flags to supplement ours as the ten of us walked the mile to the ground. It was not a pleasant experience. The decade since the clubs had last met at Hampden had dulled the memory of the worst excesses of the Rangers masses, particularly those for whom football is merely another vehicle for their snarling sectarianism.

The presence of two women in our group provided no defence to the abuse - and saliva - aimed in our direction, indeed some women eagerly joined the onslaught. Had we been draped in green, white and gold it might, at least, have been explicable - though not, of course, acceptable. With some effort we refused to succumb to the depressing reality of the punishment meted out to those who commit no greater crime than to approach a football ground from the 'wrong' direction. Indeed, we drew encouragement from the fact that United, and ourselves as the club's representatives, seemingly posed such a major threat to what the bigots regarded as theirs by right, that venom was all they had to offer in 'defence'.

The acrimony gradually subsided as we approached the National Stadium and more Arabs began to appear alongside.

Ah, Mother Hampden, born 1903, she has spawned a hundred thousand epic moments, gigantic crowds, wonder goals, dreadful mistakes, dreams fulfilled, hearts broken.... But in reality she ought to have been laid quietly to rest a decade ago, when the north stand crumbled and the ancient ash-covered terraces, long since a national disgrace, became a positive hazard to health.

But no, revamped, she lives on for some years yet. The Scottish League's recent sponsorship from B & Q must surely have been delivered in kind, judging by the patch-up job carried out, clearly with maximum 'financial efficiency'. As we approached the turnstiles, despite my long-held view that the bulldozers should have been let loose on the place, I felt some relief that the old hag was still there - it offered one more opportunity to slay the Hampden hoodoo.

The atmosphere inside the stadium hit me like a sledgehammer. We arrived about fifteen minutes before kick-off, by which time both sets of fans were in full voice. The Arabs were at least holding their own in the decibel stakes, and the thought entered my mind as I surveyed the painted faces, sea of flags and scarves and 12,000 Arabs stretching their vocal chords to the limit - what couldn't United achieve with a support like this every week?

Minutes later the noise reached a crescendo as the teams appeared; from that point the occasion forms little more than a blur in my memory.

Attempts to extract incidents and place them in chronological order have produced only the following:

* tremendous waves of emotion and encouragement rebounding from the stand roof to wash over the pitch from the United end

* the referee denying a clear penalty as Alex Cleland was sandwiched between two blue-clad bodies

* huge relief as Jim McInally stooped to make a goal-line clearance from a header (by McPherson?)

* my satisfaction with the half-time score of 0 - 0, and the belief that the longer it remained that way, the better United's chances were of creating the one goal that could win it (it seemed that was our only hope; United hadn't won a single match all season after going behind!)

* the all-important breakthrough - Rangers defence in disarray, great work by Christian Dailly, Craig Brewster's historic tap-in from what seemed like eight-and-a-half inches, and the volcanic-like eruption of tangerine and black which followed it; what also followed was my pronouncement that it was "far too early!"

For the remaining 42 minutes, the memory produces absolutely nothing other than fear - make that, horror, that Rangers' pressure would bring them an equaliser, as had happened so often in the past; in fact, not until I watched Sportscene that evening was I aware of Guido Van de Kamp's wonder stop from Mikhailitchenko, nor that, incredibly, that was the only real save he was required to make in defence of United's lead.

The minutes ticked by agonisingly slowly. Eventually, with Arabs all around on either their knees in prayer, or with their backs turned to the pitch, while the air filled with the shrill cacophony of attempts to induce the final whistle - it came.

The almighty roar which it brought from 12,000 throats contained exultation and relief in at least equal measure.

As the tears began to flow, I was certainly not immune, collapsing into my wife Lorraine's arms, rather than jumping six feet into the air. In the weeks which followed I thought often about that outpouring of emotion.

I feel not a hint of shame or embarrassment about it. It was a perfectly natural outlet for the emotion built up, not simply by the events of that historic occasion, but those of six previous Scottish Cup finals, and indeed the thirty-five year wait since my father first took me to Tannadice.

I recall, at the end of the first season, being there when United clinched promotion from the old Second Division. It was April 1960, and Jerry Kerr led them to a place in the big league after a gap of 28 years. Short trousers flapping round my knees, I joined in the pitch invasion at the final whistle and vividly remember seeing grown men around me crying, overcome with the emotion of the occasion.

I often wondered if a football match would ever evoke such a reaction in me, but until this year I had managed to withstand it. Yet there were a number of times when I might well have succumbed: beating Hearts at Hampden in 1974 to reach the Cup final for the first time; winning the League Cup in 1979 to secure the club's first-ever trophy; that never-to-be-forgotten day at Dens Park in 1983 when we clinched the League championship; the second-leg win in Moenchengladbach which took the club into the 1987 UEFA Cup final.

Historic and gut-wrenching moments one and all, and my joy at each was confined only in the respect that I remained dry of eye. For some unknown reason, none carried me that last step. But the final whistle at Hampden 1994 did, and the sight of Maurice Malpas raising aloft the old trophy, adorned with tangerine and black ribbons, set me off again!

"We're gonna celebrate" we all sang as the Cup was paraded and the players joined by Ivan Golac and those who might have been, but on the occasion were not, one of the lucky thirteen. Billy McKinlay's suspension and injuries to Scott Crabbe and Alan Main had robbed them of Cup medals, yet they joyously joined the party.

And I particularly recall the reaction of Paul Hegarty and Dave Narey, two of the finest players ever to have graced a United jersey. For both, a Scottish Cup winner's badge was the only gap in their collection of medals, caps and awards from illustrious careers. Yet, there they were, bounding around the Hampden turf, hugging everyone in sight as if they themselves had participated in this most elusive of triumphs.

Hegarty, now on the coaching staff, and Narey, who had played in earlier rounds of the Cup, but had been told (rather heartlessly, I thought) that very week that he was to be given a free transfer, celebrated for Dundee United and everyone associated with it, on and off the field - not least for us - their fellow-Arabs.

Unsurprisingly, Ivan Golac's name was chanted endlessly, his prediction having come true in stunning fashion to confound his critics and guarantee him an honoured place in the club's history. Nor was his predecessor forgotten. Jim McLean must have enjoyed the moment as much as anyone, but he steadfastly resisted the exhortations of the fans, players and backroom staff to join the celebrations on the pitch.

More than half-an-hour after the final whistle, most of us were still there, mouths bone-dry, throats hoarse, unable fully to take it all in. Somehow, it was as if leaving Hampden would end the magic, break the spell and we would all wake up from a dream to find it was really only Cup final morning!

By that time, the Rangers' supporters were back on their buses, slinking home to the four corners of Scotland, their back-to-back treble hopes shattered into a thousand pieces. What a perfect response Maurice Malpas and his team had provided to the pre-match hatred we Arabs had encountered. Dundee United were the toast of Scotland that night, glasses raised in their name by supporters of every other club in the country, relieved to learn that might isn't always right.

Back at Frixo's the drink flowed in fine style. Most of our crowd headed back to Dundee after a couple of hours for some serious celebrating, and I would happily have joined them but for a long-standing commitment to appear on BBC Radio Scotland's 'Eye to Eye' programme on Sunday morning. So for Lorraine and I, our Cup final evening celebrations were completed with a curry, then a return home in time to watch the TV highlights. I was asleep before midnight, utterly exhausted and emotionally drained.

We did make it to Dundee the next day, of course, participating in the parading of the Cup through the city and in a packed city square. It seemed incredible that the old trophy had not appeared in the city since Dundee won it in 1910, the year after the formation of the club which was to become Dundee United.

Now that United have broken their duck and laid the Hampden hoodoo to rest once and for all, it surely won't be too long before the Scottish Cup returns to Tannadice. But for me, even if a further 84 years were to elapse, in one sense it would not matter. For so long I seriously doubted whether I would ever see the Scottish Cup adorned with tangerine and black. Now, it is a memory that will live with me forever. Some of the match details may be rather vague, but the vital aspects are, and will remain, crystal clear.

21st May 1994. Dundee United 1 Rangers 0. And I was there!

It was the very best of days.

*Minnie Way*

Minnie Way was born in 1895 in Dundee. She started work in one of the jute mills when she was only twelve - a half-timer - who attended school for part of the week while she worked. She is, by her own admission, Dundee United daft, and on May 21st 1994 she sat alone in her sitting-room and watched, with tears in her eyes, as Maurice Malpas lifted the Scottish Cup.

---

# THE SECOND COMING

At ninety-nine, Minnie Way is the oldest woman in Fintry. This makes her something of a local celebrity. She has witnessed almost a century of history and her memories provide a valuable insight into the past. She's made seven documentary films with the BBC about her life and times. Minnie Way is a star, and something of an old hand when it comes to appearing on television. And, being a woman with a penchant for football, in Cup final week her sitting-room was, once again, turned into a mini television studio. In the glare of the lights she sat, in her element, beneath a photograph of the Tannadice team and talked with passion and love for her team, her favourite player – Jim McInally, and her 'skipper' – Maurice Malpas. Her face shone as she spoke. There can be no doubt that Minnie is not only one of United's oldest fans, but also one of their most ardent.

Despite the fact that Minnie has never once set foot in Tannadice, her relationship with the team is a personal one. Indeed theirs seems to be something of a mutual admiration society, for on her birthday and every Christmas, without fail, she receives a card signed by all the players. Next year she will celebrate her hundredth birthday and you can bet your life that most of the players will turn up for her party.

Despite the crippling pain of arthritis, Minnie has a prodigious gift for enjoying life and her first subject of conversation is likely to be football. And the story of the day she saw the Scottish Cup held aloft in Dundee is one of her finest.

The year is 1910. The month, April. Mary Pickford's first film is on at the cinema, whisky is 2s 10d a bottle and Minnie is all of fourteen. Dundee Football Club have won the Scottish Cup and it is to be paraded through the city. Minnie remembers it as if it were yesterday.

The city was bathed in sunshine and the centre of town was jam-packed with people from all airts and parts, many having walked in from the outlying villages to catch a glimpse of the silverware. Afraid that her daughter would get injured in the crush, Minnie's mother had forbidden her to go into the town centre, but no fourteen year old was going to miss one of the biggest parties that the city had seen. There was a carnival atmosphere and, because she and her friend were both small, they were able to push their way to the front of the throng. And when the train carrying the victorious team puffed into Dundee station there was the Cup fastened to the front of the engine! The celebrations lasted for days.

Not long afterwards, or so we are led to believe, the trophy was displayed in a local undertaker's window for all to see and admire. On seeing it there, a passing 'soothsayer' was apparently so appalled at the apparent impropriety and lack of decorum that she immediately placed a hex on the Cup saying that it would never again return to Dundee. Whether the story is apocryphal or not, it never has. Until now.

Not that Minnie Way ever believed the Cup was cursed. She pooh-poohs the idea and says that she's never been superstitious. She has always felt that it would be repossessed by one or other of the city's clubs and she never lost faith in United's ability to win it, despite suffering through all their various attempts. She confesses, however, that she was beginning to wonder if she would live to see the day. The sands of time, she says, were running out.

She's not always been fanatical about football in the interim. Indeed it was only after returning from fourteen years spent in California where she developed a taste for baseball that she took an interest in the game. And given that she'd been part of that great day in 1910 and the fact that her uncle was a mad Dundee fan, you would think that she would have had a soft spot for the Dens Parkers. But she had not the faintest inclination to support them. Indeed, she has no love for Dundee FC. She has one word for them. Skunks.

"Skunks," she says emphatically. And then tells the tale of how she came across a photograph of their Cup Winning side which was inherited, she believes, from her uncle. She decided to send it to the club. Did Dundee acknowledge her gift? They did not. And that irks Minnie. "Skunks." she repeats at the very mention of their name.

It was the Tannadice outfit that she consciously chose to support at a time when it was less usual for women to take an interest in football. But then Dundee's womenfolk are an unusual breed. Jute and jam-making, the city's traditional industries, largely employed female labour thus ensuring a certain economic independence for women. They also tended to be strong, hard-working, resilient and humorous. Minnie Way has all these qualities, and more.

She's generous by nature and in Cup final week she decided to send a gift to Maurice Malpas. So if you glimpsed a touch of lace beneath the captain's shorts on May 21st it will have been a tangerine and black garter donated by Minnie. It had been made for her but she felt she would not be able to wear something so decadent at her age, but she knew a man who might!

Eighty-four years on from Dundee FC's celebrations, United's day to lay the Cup final ghost to rest dawned in Minnie's flat. She had had a restless night. Just couldn't sleep. And getting up at sunrise just means you've longer to wait for kick-off. She couldn't settle to her usual bits and pieces of housework. She couldn't eat either and, having banned all visitors, she didn't even have the distraction of the usual steady stream of friends and neighbours. Under the circumstances they all understood. This was no day for social niceties. But the morning dragged. Eventually 12.30pm arrives and the pre-match 'rigmarole' sees Minnie stationed in front of her television and soon she's totally engrossed in it all.

Out come the teams and somehow Minnie knows that today was different from the other Cup finals she'd endured as a United fan. She could see that the players were determined to work for each other and work overtime if necessary. Mind you, there were a few heart-stopping moments and when Rangers' Dave McPherson almost scored early on in the first-half she could hardly bear to watch, but there - on the goal-line - making a lifesaving clearance was none other Jim McInally, Minnie's favourite player. "God bless Jim McInally." she says with feeling.

After that she felt less anxious and once Craig Brewster had prodded the ball into the net to secure that vital goal she knew that Rangers had had it. God bless Craigie Brewster.

As the Rangers' fans head for the exits long before the game is over she knows that the Cup will be coming back to Dundee. Nonetheless she just wishes that the referee would blow his whistle. And when he does she's crying. Crying with love and pride for her team.

God bless Ivan Golac. And God bless Jim McLean.

Looking back, eighty-four years is a long time to wait for anything, but of all the many and varied things she's seen and done Minnie is utterly convinced that this was one of the happiest days of her life. And now, she says, she can die happy. Not that Minnie Way has any intention of dying just yet. She feels that now United have broken their duck where this competition's concerned, the sky's the limit and she wants to be around to see what happens next. And then, of course, she has her hundredth birthday party to look forward to.

# LAST, BUT BY NO MEANS, LEAST

# No 1 Guido Van de Kamp

Signed from the Dutch Second Division club BVV Den Bosch for a bargain £40,000 Guido Van de Kamp was regularly to be seen in goal in his first season - 1991/92, but found it hard to claim a regular place the following season because first choice keeper, Alan Main, was in top form. When Main sustained a serious back injury in November 1993 Guido found himself once more in situ and soon became a great favourite with the United fans. He made at least two outstanding saves in the Cup final and there can be no doubt that his contribution sealed United's victory. It therefore came as something of a shock when, as soon as he had collected his Cup winner's medal and kissed the trophy, Guido picked up his P45 from Tannadice and returned to Holland to a life outside football.

---

# GUIDO'S LAST STAND

If what they say about goalkeepers is true then they are all a little crazy. Guido Van de Kamp, however, showed few signs of being the kind of mad, impetuous fool who sometimes inhabits the goalmouth. He maybe didn't have the flamboyant style of many of his ilk but his rapport with the United fans was built on firmer foundations. He was admired for his elegance and grace and loved for the conscientious way that he went about his duties and for the sense of dedication and professionalism he displayed. Guido is a thoughtful, gentle man who won the hearts of all those who supported United, most of whom considered him to be one of the finest keepers in Scotland.

And there was no occasion when he was to prove it more than on 21st May 1994 at Hampden Park. Which is perhaps a little surprising when you realise that for him this was a day of very mixed emotions. When Guido stepped out into the sunshine and pulled on his gloves, he must have been in turmoil for he knew that he had donned the number one jersey for the last time and that he was about to leave the club he had grown to love, and say goodbye to the players who had become his friends. And the even more surprising thing was that none of his teammates knew that he was preparing for his valedictory game in Scotland.

Back in Dundee his house was up for sale and all the plans had been made for his return to Holland. Only a last minute bid to resolve a contractual difficulty would make him change his mind but, given that talks had been going on since February, it seemed unlikely that there would be an eleventh hour reprieve.

From his home in Holland, where he now works in his uncle's business, Guido talks of his last game. He says that the 21st May was perhaps the best day of his life, and then quickly corrects himself by saying that it was the best day of his playing career. The recent birth of his baby daughter, Lotte, was, not surprisingly, just that little bit more special and meaningful!

"I was determined to go out on a high. If this was to be my last game I wanted it to be a memorable one. I desperately wanted to keep a clean sheet." And, despite the efforts of the most expensive strikeforce in Scottish football, he fulfilled his last ambition. His save, in the second-half from an Alexei Mikhailitchenko shot, was world class and hugely significant to the outcome of the game.

"I always felt that we might just win the Cup. Everything seemed to point to it, right from the first game at Arbroath we seemed to work together and get stronger with every match. Every match was tough and we had more than our fair share of troubles along the way. The Motherwell replay at Fir Park stands out particularly - first I had had to play for most of the ninety minutes with a dislocated finger and then Scott Crabbe broke his leg. Nothing was easy - but we had the strength and tenacity to overcome such things - and Brian Welsh's goal proved that."

And Welsh was to come to Van de Kamp's rescue in the semi-final against Aberdeen when, with only minutes remaining, he scored from a close-range header which took the tie to a replay after an uncharacteristic mistake by the keeper had given the opposition the impression that they were on their way to the final.

And when it came to mistakes, Ivan Golac's philosophy served to give the team resilience. Rather than dwelling on the negative aspects of the game he would simply say that everyone makes mistakes and for Guido this kind of thinking gave him the confidence to feel stronger. "It made you look forward and not backwards."

And looking forward is the goalkeeper's lot in life. Distanced from the goalscoring action of his team-mates his is a lonely vigil, a fact which Guido recognises. "You are never really part of the celebrations, even if you jump around a bit you can't get too carried away - you'd feel a bit of a fool, but it doesn't mean that you aren't just as emotional and involved. But Craig Brewster's goal in the Cup final was so important I didn't care how foolish I looked!"

The whole game was special for the player; his parents and other members of his family had travelled from Holland to watch him, and the fact that they had been denied the chance to see him play on a regular basis gave him an added incentive to perform well. He recalls how amazed he was to arrive at the stadium on the team bus and see the crowd gathered in the car park - fans and press all held back by barriers and police and suddenly, there before him, was his father - out of all those people his father had managed to get through in time to wish his son luck before the game. It was a moving experience for both men.

Apart from the memories and photographs which help him relive the day, being a Cup winner has its advantages even in Holland. "Although I haven't signed for a club over here I train with my old club, Den Bosch, and everyone has much more respect for you because they know that you played in such an important game."

"It goes without saying," he concludes, "that I still miss everyone at United and all the fans."

Not half as much as we miss you, Guido. Not half as much!

# No 2 Alex Cleland

Born in Glasgow in 1970, Alex Cleland joined the club as a schoolboy and has now claimed the number two shirt as his own. He's made well over a hundred appearances in it and, like most of the longer-serving members of the United squad, has played for Scotland at Under-21 level. Despite having twice broken his leg he is one of the cornerstones of United's defence. In many ways Cleland represents an ideal - the embodiment of the present and the hope for the future. In the Cup final he was detailed to keep tabs on Gordon Durie - no easy assignment.

---

# ON DURIE DUTY

If ever the words 'unsung hero' could be more aptly used to describe a player it would be Alex Cleland. Week in and week out he patrols the right flank with such efficiency and dedication that people just tend to take his contribution for granted. Others tend to catch the eye and the headlines. Perhaps it's because Cleland is honest, unaffected and modest, and never flashy, that the media are inclined to ignore him. Not the Tannadice fans though - they sing his praises every week. Perhaps just not loudly enough.

Essentially an attacking right-back, he can ghost along the touchline with the greatest of ease, overlapping to help a team-mate - or simply running with the ball himself. He can send in a cross with accuracy, or sneak in behind defences to make a surprise appearance in the box to pick up the ball. Versatile and brave, a player without malice.

Cleland's instructions on 21st May were something along the lines of: "Keep Gordon Durie quiet. Get forward as much as you can, but make sure Durie has no freedom." Simple! There was Alexander Cleland - with his boyish looks, twenty-three years old, 5'8" and a bit, just over eleven stones, who signed for United as a schoolboy; and there was Gordon Scott Durie - one of the grown-ups, twenty-eight, taller and almost two stones heavier than Cleland, formerly of Chelsea and Spurs and now making a name for himself at Ibrox. Easy peasy!

Not that the two players were strangers. This was something of a revenge match for the United man; on a previous occasion Durie had twice escaped from Cleland to score. Cleland was determined this would be no repeat performance. "As the game went on I felt I was getting the better of him and when, on one occasion, I got to the ball before him and he got really annoyed I knew I was in the driving seat."

It was a day when defenders needed to be the driving force in the game - and in many ways it was won in defence. With goalscorers of the quality of Hateley, Durie and McCoist, Cleland and his co-defenders needed to be in top form.

United's success, the player agrees, was all about confidence. "The mood amongst the players was just so relaxed that no-one contemplated defeat. Even on the way to Hampden," he says, "we were all in high spirits." And much of the credit for the pre-match optimism Cleland believes must go to Billy McKinlay. "On the bus 'Badger' was terrific, he just joked and laughed the whole way to the ground - it kept everyone's mind off the game. I don't know how he did it, he must have been feeling so down and disappointed and yet he was so supportive."

And when the sound of the final whistle had long-since died, the medals had been presented, the fans had all drifted away from the ground and the party was just getting into full swing in the dressingroom, Cleland suddenly heard the doctor telling him that he was to put down his drink and go and sit, in splendid isolation. He and Gordan Petric had been selected for the obligatory drugs test. And there they stayed until 8.00pm. Gordan had had the good sense to change into his mufti, while Alex was still in his strip. Their companions for the sojourn - David Robertson and Alexei Mikhailitchenko. "We passed the time chatting about the game, and both the Rangers' players conceded that the better team had won - so there were no sour grapes."

And did his late arrival in Dundee put a damper on the whole affair? "Not for long. We soon made up for lost time!"

## No 3 Maurice Malpas

To most United fans Maurice Malpas is a God. Mr Dependable. His reputation goes before him. There is no better or more conscientious defender in the Premier Division, a fact that is born out by glancing at the record of his international career. At 32, and with more than fifty appearances for his country, Malpas is one of that select group in Scotland's Hall of Fame. He joined United in 1979 as a schoolboy and has now played well over six hundred games in tangerine and is, of course, Captain of the side. And when Mo went up to lift the Scottish Cup there is no doubt that this was one of the most moving experiences of his Tannadice career.

---

# THROUGH THE EYES OF A CHILD...

Little Darren Malpas is unlikely to forget the 1994 Cup final. When his mother lifted him down to the pitch at the end of the ninety minutes he must have thought he was at the biggest party in the world. Imagine being seven and standing beside your Dad at Hampden in front of twelve thousand jubilant fans, half of them in fancy dress. Imagine seeing your Dad hold up the Scottish Cup and hearing his name ring out all over Mount Florida. And then, with the wide-eyed innocence of youth, Darren followed his Dad into the dressingroom and could have been forgiven for thinking he had entered a madhouse. There were all the players, men he probably knew as responsible adults, drinking champagne, spraying it over one another, kissing and cuddling and generally behaving... well.. like a bunch of seven year-olds! In the midst of all the mayhem the club doctor was going round giving preventative injections to all and sundry for their forthcoming trip to Trinidad. And when the door opened and some of the directors came through it Darren fully expected there to be an almighty row. But sometimes grown-ups are full of surprises. If Darren and his chums had been up to such antics he was sure his Dad would have had a thing or two to say about their behaviour, and undoubtedly the word 'childish' would have passed his lips. But instead he hears his Dad saying, "When you've just won the Scottish Cup, you can do anything!"

Even at seven Darren Malpas must realise that his Dad is no ordinary footballer for Maurice is one of the few players that Scotland has produced who plays the game as it should be played. He's a man of such composure that when he's on the ball he looks as though he has all the time in the world to decide just what to do with it. Not for him the hopeful hurried punt up the park. In the grim business of defending Darren's Dad is more than just a stopper, he's playmaker as well. To him a football pitch and the players on it are like a chess board and pieces, and the match a game of strategy. He knows the worth of the men around him, their strengths and their weaknesses. As soon as his job is done at the back he's quite likely to sail forward to set up an attack, bringing others into the game with well-placed passes.

This was Malpas' fifth Cup final - three times he has captained the side - and if what they say about losing being character building is true then all those failed dreams certainly served to make him more determined to win it this time. And it showed.

Amazingly the player says that, despite the results on previous occasions, he would have been loathe to miss any of the finals, while at the same time he admits that the 1987 game against St Mirren is still a source of pain. "We played so badly, and then to go on and lose the UEFA Cup days later makes that whole period something of a nightmare."

This time, he says, the pressure was off United. They might have been the people's choice to win on the day, but once again, with dreary predictability, all the pundits and supposed cognoscenti had their money on the opposition. Surprise, surprise. But Malpas knew there was an inherent vulnerability about Rangers, their recent run of results didn't bear close scrutiny, and the very fact that they were chasing an Ibrox record must have made then doubly nervous. In fact, he says, the longer the game went on the more nervous they became. "Clearly they thought that they would score a couple of goals early on, have it all wrapped up by half-time, and the rest of the game would be a stroll. And suddenly the master plan was going wrong."

When you ask him if being Captain in such games brings added burdens he'll reply that his responsibilities are much the same as on other occasions, with the one bonus - if you win you get to lift the trophy! This time, however, along with the other members of the Dundee United Scottish Cup Veterans Association (Dave Bowman and Jim McInally), he was subjected to a lot more media interest than the rest of the players. And of course, as is the way of journalists, dear sweet things that they are, they simply had to remind him of Hampden's hoodoo. But Malpas pooh-poohed all such talk. "As far I was concerned Hampden held no fears. I'd played there in manys a winning side." (What do you mean, When? When he played for Scotland, of course!)

Words fail him when he tries to describe his feelings when he actually got his hands on that most elusive of trophies. Relief? Well, yes, there was a bit of that. Joy? Certainly, but it, too, seems somewhat inadequate to describe his feelings. And that old cliché - over the moon - is far from appropriate. In the final analysis he'll agree that only those who were there will know exactly just how special that moment was.

# No 4 Jim McInally

There is no more honest player in Scottish football than Jim McInally. He is one of the good guys - an extremely personable player who always has time for the fans. Glasgow-born he played for Celtic, Dundee, Nottingham Forest and Coventry City before signing for United. To date he has made well over 250 appearances for the club and has never given less than a hundred percent effort in every one of those games. McInally has a knack of scoring against Aberdeen and, true to form, he did just that in the semi-final replay - a goal which took United through to the final.

---

# TRUE GRIT

When all the odds are against you and few believe that you can win, it's then that character and personality count. If ever Ivan Golac needed men of steel and true grit it was in the Cup final, and he had to look no further than Jim McInally to find these qualities.

Right from the start in this game United achieved what they set out to do: to cramp Rangers' midfield style, to hustle them and prevent them from building the platform of authority from which to launch the total destruction so widely and confidently forecast. That it never happened owed much to the men in United's midfield, to Jim McInally et al.

When McInally tries to analyse what playing in the final meant to him on a personal level he states simply and unequivocally that it was the most important game of his life. "At my age, you can't afford to be blasé about games like this because at the back of your mind you're always wondering if you'll ever make it to another Cup final."

And history, he believes, is an important factor in football. A place in the history books is well worth having for it provides immortality for the footballer - and that's a precious thing. Having arrived at the club in 1986, McInally has always had to live in the shadow of the 1982/83 Championship-winning side - and sometimes comparisons made him feel like a loser. Not long before the final, he had attended a dinner given in honour of the League winners. He remarked then that the next time they were gathered together he hoped that it would be to fête a new set of winners - and now all he has to do is wait for the invitation!!

Losing this game just didn't bear thinking about. The pain of the Motherwell defeat still makes him wince. "I was so determined to win in 1991 and the disappointment of losing, and the fact that I was sent off in the tunnel afterwards, left such a bitter taste."

This time, though, everything was perfect. "I love horse racing, and when we went to Hamilton racecourse the day before the game it was too good to be true. Then later that night we were involved in making 'Sportscene' and I believe that many of the doubters who saw us on the programme may have been convinced that this time we could do it. We had a long chat before the game and it was clear that every player was determined to prove a lot of people wrong. The manager instilled in us the notion that we were good enough to win and much of the credit must be put down to Ivan whose man-management skills are second to none."

McInally remembers the game itself as one which he found exhausting - both mentally and physically and yet, like the other players, he found that the ninety minutes were over in a trice. He recalls that when United were denied a penalty in the early stages he just thought that maybe their luck was out. The decision to play on made him angry. "I was ready to fight the world."

But by half-time his anger had subsided, and in the dressingroom he was strengthened by the feeling in the camp that, by not allowing Rangers to score and by playing some clever football themselves, half the battle had been won.

And what of the goal? "I'm always aware of the fans, and when we scored I thought that after the initial delirium our crowd went a little quiet and then I realised that they knew, like we did, what was coming. We all braced ourselves for the onslaught. And although it came, the Rangers' fans were none too happy with their team's performance and they were starting to give them a really hard time, which put more pressure on them which, in turn, helped us."

When finally the game was over McInally, spotting journalist Hugh Keevins on the sidelines, threw himself into his arms - a fact which did not go unnoticed by Archie MacPherson during his radio commentary of the game who told his listeners that Hugh Keevins was dancing up and down in celebration with Jim McInally. Jim laughs, "In actual fact, the press are supposed to be neutral - and I don't know whether Hugh is a United supporter or not - he didn't have much choice in the matter, I just grabbed him."

All in all it was a day that the player wanted to experience and savour to the full, so when afterwards, in the dressingroom, the champagne was flowing and drink was plentiful there came a point when he took the conscious decision to stay sober - just so that he could remember every last minute of the day.

And does he? "Down to the most minute detail. An experience like that is difficult to forget. It keeps you going through the bad times!"

## *No 5 Gordan Petric*

Ivan Golac made the signing of fellow-countryman Gordan Petric his number one priority when he arrived at Tannadice. He'd managed him at Partizan Belgrade and made no secret of his admiration for the big defender. Petric cost United the record sum of £650,000, but it was money well spent. Still only twenty-five, Petric is one of the coolest, classiest players this side of the Border, qualities which earned him Man of the Match in the Cup final.

---

# SIMPLY THE BEST

Contrary to popular belief, experience isn't everything in football. Gordan Petric is the living proof of this. He was a mere boy of nineteen when he made his international debut at Wembley against England. Few footballers who play in defence can have been selected for their country whilst still in their teens. But Petric is no ordinary footballer.

Pete Sampras lookalike, Petric, was something of an unknown quantity to the United fans before his arrival but it took only a matter of minutes for them to realise that here was someone who was in a class of his own. A veritable giant amongst players, he has the kind of physique that goalkeepers would die for. At 6'3" his arms seem to brush the ground and his hands are huge. But Petric is a sweeper - a leader, a fighter, a strategist and a creator. He has elegance and intelligence - and it is, most would agree, a great privilege to watch him play.

He makes even the best of opposing strikers look foolish at times, robbing them of the ball with such apparent ease and very little effort that they are left bewildered and confused.

The sweeper has a more complex role than the orthodox defender. He needs to be a very knowledgeable player, a good all-rounder and someone who can read the pattern of the game and understand isolated situations as well. Because he is usually responsible for an area, rather than a player, it's not a job every player can do. And you watch Gordan Petric, always on the move, marking the ball, men and the space - always adjusting, never hurried, never 'puffed', and you know he's a master craftsman. He's brilliant.

And what, one wonders, enticed a player of his obvious talents to Dundee United. After all, he was quite accustomed to playing before huge audiences in Yugoslavia. A crowd of almost 100,000 was not unusual for a game played between Partizan and Red Star at the latter club's Crvena Zvezda Stadium; and even Partizan's ground, JNA, holds over 47,000. A far cry from Tannadice. An even further cry from Arbroath's Gayfield where United started their Cup campaign. And the chance to win a trophy or two can't have been the main attraction either, for he has won eight - one for every year of his career. So when you ask Petric what attracted him to Scotland, he tells you that he has always loved British football. "Ivan Golac knew me as a player, he also knew that I wanted to play in Britain." He had had tempting offers from other clubs. "I'd been approached by German club, Nuremberg, and by Lyon in France, but I was happy to come to Dundee United and to work with Ivan again."

And in one respect Dundee reminds him of home. The close proximity of Tannadice to Dens Park is not unlike the situation in Belgrade. "Partizan and Red Star are only a few hundred yards apart. A five minute stroll."

Gordan Petric believes that United have great potential. "It is a young side, and if we play together for a couple of years we are capable of great things." And he's quickly got the measure of Scottish football. "Rangers and Celtic may be the big clubs here - they can afford to buy three or four good players every year. Clubs like United have to rely on a different approach, they have to hold on to players and try to build a good team." He also has kind words for the United fans. "The supporters are very loyal. They turn up even when the results are bad because they have a good relationship with the players - they are 'protective' of them."

The Cup final was special for Petric. His calm authority throughout the ninety minutes gave the defence a look of invincibility. "The first trophy I won was in Chile when I played for my country in the Under-21 side, eight years ago. It was very special because it came at the start of my career. I could tell that the Scottish Cup meant a lot to everyone at United. For me to win it in my first season here felt much the same as winning that first one, it marked the start of my career in Scotland, my first British trophy."

And certainly not his last!

## No 6 Brian Welsh

Alongside Gordan Petric, Brian Welsh has formed one of the most potentially exciting defensive pairings in the Premier Division. He's only 25, but caught the eye with his performances not only in the Cup final, and the run up to it, but throughout the whole of the season. Born in Edinburgh he signed for United from Tynecastle Boys Club in 1985 and made his first League appearance in the season 1986/87. However he was unable to claim a regular place in the team until the arrival of Ivan Golac, but just seems to have gone from strength to strength since then.

---

# THE MAN WHO HAD MARK HATELEY IN HIS POCKET

Time was a manager, in search of centre-back, went out into the street and signed the first chap who could tackle like an earth-mover and kicked the ball as if he hated it with every fibre of his being. Nowadays such Neanderthals have given way to the all-purpose footballer who can create as well as destroy, win matches as well as save them. And in these respects Brian Welsh fits the bill.

He's both safe and sure at the back. Every so often he'll make an appearance in the penalty box; on these occasions you can almost see him saying to himself 'If no-one else is going to score then I'd better go up and give them a hand.' And off he sets. Once inside his opponents' area, large and imposing, waiting for the corner or the free-kick, his presence alone is enough to cause consternation. He can jump to such a height that it makes you doubt Newton's theories on gravity. It was on two such missions into the box that Welsh came to score a couple of goals which may well turn out to be the most important of his career. The first, as we all know, was the winner in the fourth round replay at Fir Park against Motherwell - a right-footed strike which looked for all the world as though it would break the netting. The second was his eleventh-hour header which provided the equaliser in the semi-final against Aberdeen.

"After scoring against Motherwell I was absolutely determined that we weren't going to be knocked out of the competition in the semi-final so as the game went on I knew I had to keep getting into scoring positions in the hope I could get the equaliser."

Welsh is a very different player to the one he was in previous years. Naturally unassuming, he was constantly riddled with self-doubt. He found it hard to believe in his own ability. But confidence is a wonderful thing and once he secured a regular place in the team he began to blossom and, as they say, has never looked back since. He continues to grow in stature.

Not that he has ever lacked height. He stands 6'2" in his stocking soles, although sometimes you'd swear he was 8'9". Not for nothing is he called 'Big' Welshie. But size isn't everything and in the final he showed that he was not only dominant in the air, but that he could outwit even the cleverest of opponents - a fact to which Mark Hateley will no doubt testify - unwillingly!

How can we ever forget how Welshie subdued Hateley for almost the full ninety minutes of play. He had him in his pocket. Quite literally, for Scott Crabbe had given him a picture of the Rangers' striker and he kept it in his top pocket - producing it at the drop of a hat every time Hateley's name came up in conversation.

And, as it turns out, Hateley was very much the instrument of his own destruction. On hearing the Rangers' player say, in a radio interview, as he expounded on his many and indubitable qualities, that a defender only has a good game when he himself has a bad one, Welsh immediately interpreted the words 'a defender' as 'Brian Welsh'. It made him livid. "Most people believed that if Mark Hateley was allowed to play then Rangers would win. I knew I had to keep him under control and prove not only to the crowd, but to Hateley himself, that he had a bad game when I had a good one." And he did, it seems, prove his point for at the end of the match Hateley came up and patted him on the shoulder.

And did the prospect of taking on the most potent force in Scottish football ever seem daunting in the anticipation. Not, apparently, until the morning of the game and then the player suddenly was suddenly stricken with a bout of nervousness. He couldn't sleep, he felt sick and had difficulty eating. However, when he arrived at the ground and was greeted by all the well-wishers, and later the encouragement of the United fans throughout the game, both helped to dispel his fears and sustain him through to the final whistle.

## No. 7 Dave Bowman

Signed from Coventry City along with Jim McInally for the bargain deal of £140,000, Dave Bowman's Tannadice career has stretched over eight years. He is the son of Hearts' favourite, Andy Bowman, and at the tender age of eighteen Dave captained the Edinburgh side - their youngest ever skipper. His energy and vision have made him one of the most feared, and respected, midfielders in the business. In the 1991 Cup final he was Man of the Match, a performance that was to earn him his first international cap, but even that was not recompense enough for losing at Hampden. Dave Bowman has paid his dues in this competition and nothing in his career has probably ever tasted as sweet as winning this trophy on the eighth anniversary of his arrival at Dundee United.

---

# DAVIE BOWMAN'S SMILE

Not a soul could deny that Dundee United were deserved Cup winners. Their technique, agility and anticipation were a match and more for Rangers; their hearts and lungs as big. And of all the players on the field there was none more committed, more dynamic, than Dave Bowman. He was an essential, integral part of the side and at times it seemed he would willingly have played single-handed.

Bowman is a winner, this was his crusade and woe betide anyone who, in the preceding days and weeks, talked about the Cup final in his hearing and mentioned the dreaded f-word. Failure was not to be part anyone's vocabulary. He simply couldn't bear to contemplate losing.

And although his mood fluctuated between optimism and deep despair in actual fact, in the run-up to it he tried hard not to think about the game at all. When he did he says he was overwhelmed by the desire to win this trophy, not only to end the hoodoo but also before the time came to exchange his boots for a pair of carpet slippers! "I don't mind admitting I was scared that this would be my last chance to win something - you don't get many opportunities like this over the years, and the older you get the more worried you become that the really big ones are always going to pass you by."

On previous occasions, against less favoured teams, the general expectation was that United would lift the trophy and those players who had been there, and lost, will never forget the dashed hopes and the debilitating effect that the whole experience had on them. "All summer you just kept looking back at the game and mulling it over and over in your mind. I don't imagine that some of the younger players in the team, and those who had just arrived at the club, fully appreciate just what they have been involved in this time around. Maybe in years to come it will hit them, but this was my fourth final and, believe me, winning this one - after all that pain - was so special, especially when you think that some exceptional players go through their whole careers without winning anything."

And Bowman reckons that Ivan Golac's approach to the game was a major factor in their victory. "He told us that he felt Rangers didn't want to play us. That we were their bogey team. And you could see some of the players thinking, maybe they don't want to play us, after all we had beaten them 3 - 0 at Ibrox only a matter of months before, so maybe we did have a psychological advantage. And by the time we arrived at Hampden we were confident that we could give them a run for their money. And we did!"

A subscriber to the doesn't-time-fly-when-you're-enjoying yourself school of thought, the game, for him, is something of a blur. "It all passed so quickly - one minute it was kick-off the next we were lifting the trophy - or so it seemed. After we scored it did seem to slow down somewhat - I remember asking Jimmy Mac how much time was left at one point - he told me there were still twenty minutes on the clock and then before I knew it Dougie Hope was telling me that there were only two minutes left to play."

"At the finish I just grabbed Jimmy and we seemed to be stuck together for hours. I knew that of all the players he would know just how I was feeling. I remember, too, looking up into the stand and seeing my Dad and my sister, Sarah, and realising that they too were overcome with emotion."

"The celebrations at the end were the best I've ever experienced. Mind you, I might easily have been arrested for, when Ricky Ross ran onto the trackside and I raced to meet him, the police were quick to try to separate us. One of the policeman told me that I should know better - but I just asked him how he came to that conclusion, after all I'd never won the Cup before!"

And if there is ever testimony to just how much this meant to the player - just look at the photographs - that grin, it just speaks volumes.

## *No. 8 David Hannah*

Born in Coatbridge in 1974 David Hannah is a reminder to everyone of just how effective Dundee United's youth policy is. There is nothing more rewarding for the fans than to watch a youngster graduate though the ranks until he becomes a fully-fledged professional. Already Hannah's international career has seen him play both at youth and under-21 level and a call-up to the full squad must now be only a matter of time. He made his debut in the season before last and has now established himself as a regular in midfield. Nonetheless he is a perfectionist who is constantly trying to improve his game. The Cup final proved to be his showcase and has established him as a household name.

---

# THE TRIUMPH OF YOUTH...

Sensible. Now there's a word not usually associated with footballers. Particularly the younger ones. But in David Hannah's case it's the first one that springs to mind. At 21 he seems wise beyond his years. He is clearly very dedicated to his sport and greatly respected by fellow professionals and fans. Added to this, he is also extremely likeable.

Arguably one of the most precocious talents at Tannadice it is clear that no-one threatens a more emphatic midfield dominance than he does. Already he is almost the complete player and the worst that you can say of him is that he lacks experience. Hannah's feet, however, are planted firmly on the ground. At Tannadice, to be precise. While others may have itchy feet this boy is quite content to stay put for the moment. He believes that the talent and experience to be found amongst United's coaching staff is unmatched in Scottish football and that what success he has had to date can be attributed to three men. Jim McLean, he says, always believed in him and has continually encouraged him to improve his game. Ivan Golac has given him confidence, "He tells us to have a touch of arrogance when we play - it helps self-belief and makes the opposition wary of you." And Paul Hegarty, he says, has taught him so much about the game that he feels his breakthrough from the reserves to the first team is largely due to the coaching he has had from Hegarty throughout his career. Following this train of thought to its logical conclusion, Hannah believes that it is largely due to Heggie's guidance and expertise that he made an appearance in the Cup Final.

When in 1991 he watched, from his sick bed, as United failed in their bid to beat Motherwell, little did he think that three years later not only would he be playing in another final, but that he would also be in a winning side. "You always believe that you'll win a trophy or two during your playing days, but to win one when you are still only twenty is very exciting."

Hannah knows that there was a lot of pressure on him to play well. "With Billy McKinlay suspended there were quite a few who thought that we couldn't win without him and that I was a very poor substitute for a player with 'Badger's' flair and vision. I knew I had to prove them wrong."

He talks about the build-up to the match and, like the other players, he too felt relaxed. "I tried not to think too much about the actual game. I found other distractions. I went along to Deacon Blue's farewell concert during the previous week - I also went to see the film 'Four Weddings and a Funeral'." An early night on the Friday night and there was no doubt that he was in the right frame of mind for the game.

"When we all walked out onto the pitch at Hampden there was this unmistakable feeling that we could beat Rangers. No-one said anything, but we could all feel it. There they were, going for the treble for the second year in a row, with a side where two of their cheaper players probably cost more than the whole of our team, but they were the ones who seemed a little anxious. In fact, when we were warming-up I was very aware that they were watching us - probably to see if we were at all unnerved by them and their fans. It must have unnerved them a little to see that we weren't!"

In the end, Hannah puts United's success down to two things. Determination and team-work. "The players all played for one another and every department functioned as a unit."

To have played in such a game was a tremendous experience for Hannah. It was, he reckons, not only rewarding for each player but it was good for the team as a whole. And anything, he says, which halts the domination of Scottish football by Rangers is good for the game in general.

At the end of the game he remembers looking over at his mentor, Paul Hegarty, and wondering what he must have been feeling, to have been at Hampden so many times before and not won - and now he was only able to experience the joy of victory secondhand. Hannah also looked round for his father - the man who had guided and supported him throughout his career and saw to his amazement that his father, bursting with pride at his son's achievement, had tears in his eyes.

He wasn't the only one.

# No 9 Andy McLaren

Ask any true football fan what his/her favourite type of player is and nine times out of ten, if he or she has a soul, they'll reply 'a winger'. Dundee United rarely play without one, and often play with two. Now that's the height of luxury. And when the winger in question is Andy McLaren there'll be moments in the game when you'll hold your breath in anticipation. And in the Cup final the whole nation held its breath every time he touched the ball. He's an under-21 internationalist who made his debut for United three seasons ago when he was only 18.

---

# A DREAM COME TRUE? NOT QUITE...

The rise to fame of this gallus Glasgow boy has been another of the success stories associated with the Tannadice youth training scheme! His raw precocious talent first beguiled those who saw him play in the youth side, then he became the toast of the reserves and now he relishes playing before larger crowds. Working with the touchline close to their elbows there's not much space for wingers to strut their stuff, so when they shuffle and sway, inviting their opponents to make the wrong decision, it makes you nervous and excited. It is sheer artistry. McLaren is the archetypal winger - an artful dodger who torments and teases opponents.

This is a boy who simply loves football and who is so comfortable with the ball that just watching him playing keepie-uppie in the warm-up is sheer pleasure. He can keep a football up in the air on instep, thigh and head from breakfast to lunchtime. He wants the ball for the whole ninety minutes playing time and should his team-mates neglect to present it to him for a spell, he's quite likely to go in the huff!

And you'd think from his demeanour that if ever there was a late night reveller with a penchant for the bright lights it would be McLaren. But you'd be wrong. Off the field he's quiet, nervous. He rarely frequents Dundee's night-spots, preferring instead to stay in and watch a good film, restless to play his next game and looking forward to the days when he can head 'down the road' to Glasgow to see his girlfriend and his mother.

McLaren has ambition and intelligence, but admits he was never all that keen on school. He reckons that, coming from an area of high unemployment, if circumstances had been different he could easily have ended up on the dole - or even in jail - like many of his contemporaries. He saw football as an escape route. He knew he had to make it. He thought he could.

And watching Andy McLaren at Hampden you knew he had come of age. He was in his element on such a big stage, his exuberance giving him extra guile. He admits that no-one talked about defeat before the game. The word was taboo. No-one even looked scared which, he says, was half the battle. He even relished playing against Rangers. "If you won against them, then no-one could say it was a fluke, and if you lost, well, at least you had gone out to a team that everyone thought would win it anyway."

Prior to the game there were no sleepless nights for McLaren, no pacing the floor in the wee small hours, and in his dreams he always scored the winning goal. "I must have scored at least ten winners in the days leading up to the match. I shared a room with Brian Welsh and every morning he used to ask me how many goals I'd scored during the night!"

But the dream never quite materialised. "I remember at one point in the game I was standing at the back post on my own and Christian was coming in on the far side with the ball - I was screaming at him to send it over, but he sent it to the front post instead. That seemed to be my one wee chance for glory. Not", he hastens to add, "that it matters, for the whole day was a dream."

# No 10 Craig Brewster

In 1976, when Craig Brewster was only ten, he started training with United. He had been spotted by two eagle-eyed scouts, and that's when his love affair with the club began. First and foremost he was a fan who, like the rest of us, probably dreamt that one day he would score a goal or two in tangerine. Imagine his dismay when, having signed as a schoolboy, the club released him. Cast into exterior darkness he found himself some part-time work and played Junior football. From that he joined Forfar and six and a half years on he signed for Raith Rovers where his goalscoring feats were soon the talk of Kirkcaldy and parts beyond. Partly due to Brewster's prowess, Jimmy Nicholl's side found themselves in the Premier Division and Craig Brewster found himself back at Tannadice.

---

## LOCAL HERO

Craig Brewster is no ordinary goalscorer. He can turn the half-chance into a spectacular goal in the twinkling of an eye. Having got off to something of a false start with United when he first signed, he is now idolised by the fans who think that if he's within shooting distance of the goal he might just have a go. 'Walking in a Brewster Wonderland' is nonsense song No 1 in their repertoire. (And if young Robbie Winters starts scoring, we might be the only fans who will be able to get the title almost right!) Certainly some of the goals Brewster has scored have been out of the ordinary. In actual fact he'll shoot from any distance and with either foot. Of course he gets it wrong now and again but his whole game is based on the premiss that a striker's got to be prepared to miss otherwise he'll never have a go.

And he wasn't always in the forefront of play. It was manager, Jimmy Nicholl, who transformed him from a midfielder into a striker, a move which paid off handsomely for Raith Rovers. And even to this day Jimmy Nicholl mourns his loss. Brewster, too, has fond memories of his two years with Nicholl and while he has no regrets about signing for United, he admits he owes a great deal to Nicholl and all his former team-mates.

It was a relaxed Craig Brewster who prepared to play in the Cup final. Ivan Golac's laid-back approach again rubbing off on the player. "There were no restrictions on us. We were told to spend the preceding days doing more or less what we liked . Happily I bumped into a chap who was the club captain at East Kilbride Golf Course and so I spent the Friday pottering about on the golf course."

Brewster agrees that having not played in any of the previous Cup final defeats, and not being associated with the club other than as a fan, he arrived at the final without any of the 'baggage' that might have made him nervous. "I'd never lost at Hampden, it held no real fears and because Rangers had had a bad couple of months I knew that with a bit of luck we could do it. And after the first ten minutes or so of play I just felt that we really were going to pull it off. There were no weak links in the team and even without Billy McKinlay the midfield held together so well. Davie Hannah was outstanding." High praise indeed from the man who was quite outstanding himself!

Of the goal he says much of the praise must go to Christian Dailly for masterminding it. But Brewster was the man who put it in the back of the net and there can be few experiences in life like scoring the winning goal in a National Cup final. To see your club's name etched on the trophy and know that you helped put it there; to know that although you may be the most unpopular person in certain parts of Glasgow, elsewhere in Scotland you had become an icon; to hear the Hampden roar ring out in the Mount Florida air and hear you name sung by 12,000 voices must have been one of the most exhilarating experiences imaginable. "Correct." says Brewster.

"I look back and can see it all so vividly. I remember flicking the ball on to Christian and then watching as he pressurised McPherson and Maxwell. And then as the ball hit off Christian I thought I'd just keep on running in on goal in the hope that something would turn up." His Micawberism paid off. The ball rolled in front of goal, hit the post and who should be there to thump in the rebound? None other than Craigie Brewster. Cue the rapturous applause.

And there he stood, looking up into the crowd as 12,000 delirious souls danced, waved and clasped one another with incredulous delight. He stood engulfed in the monstrous roar which swelled and boomed and rolled down onto the pitch and then up, up and out over Glasgow.

A great, great moment.

# No 11 Christian Dailly

Dundee born and Tannadice bred, Christian Dailly, seems to have been around for such a long time that it is hard to believe that he is barely out of his teens. He made his debut when he was just 16 and the remarkable thing is that he made the transition from the youth team to the first team without playing in the reserves. He is also that rare kind of player - a fan of the club he plays for - his stock answer to the question 'What would you be doing on a Saturday if you didn't play for United?' is 'Watching them.' Dailly's role in the Cup final was crucial - but for his quick-thinking actions there might have been no victory....

---

# CHRISTIAN AID

Some say that Christian Dailly is too nice, too gentle to be a footballer. Maybe so, but it's not only the mad, showy players who are effective and exciting, the game needs its thoughtful, clever players just as much. Probably more so. Dailly is elegant and cultured, he has pace, style and some lovely touches, all of which set him above the average player. He is also exceedingly diffident and unassuming, dislikes watching himself on television and shies away from interviews wherever possible. He hates it when he's not playing well and you get the impression that he's prone to bouts of self-doubt. He'll tell you that he doesn't think he's a natural goalscorer, he has to work hard at it. Being tall and strong he invites the long, high ball when it is abundantly clear that he is happier with it at his feet where he can take on defenders and bamboozle them en route to the net. Recently he has played as a surrogate midfielder, but it was his surprise appearances in defence which really wowed the Tannadice crowd. The truth is you just never know where Dailly is going to turn up next.

Clearly academic, the player sometimes regrets the fact that he never went to university and envies some of his friends who are students. Then he quietly informs you that he is doing an Open University degree. In his spare time Christian Dailly studies maths and physics - that's when he's not changing nappies - for he has recently become a father!

Cup final day found Christian more relaxed than he believed possible. "I just adopted the attitude that I was going to have a good time. Even if I had a poor game and had to be substituted I'd still have played in a final at Hampden - and that's more than many players have done." Mind you he did spend most of the morning trying to get a ticket for his cousin who had somehow misplaced his original one. Tickets were like gold dust and his quest was fruitless, still it served to take his mind off the afternoon's work.

Rangers were there to be beaten, seems to have been the consensus of opinion in the team. Thinking with which Christian concurs. Hope, he believed, would triumph over experience. "From the moment I walked out onto the pitch I realised that the fans really believed in us. You'd never have known that they were outnumbered, they were there to have a good time, I remember looking at all the daft things people were wearing and thinking that no-one looked as though they were going to a funeral. The Rangers end was just so still in comparison - it gave me, what I can only describe as, a tremendous buzz. Instead of being awestruck by the whole affair, I just wanted to take it all in."

And the goal? When history records that it was scored by Craig Brewster it will only tell half the story. Lest anyone forgets, Christian created it. Without Dailly's speed of thought and presence of mind Brewster wouldn't have scored. Without Brewster's opportunistic eye and his tenacity Dailly's cross would have bounced harmlessly away from the target. It was a joint effort.

Christian's memories clearly show that the goal was no fluke. The backpass? "When McPherson sent the ball back towards the keeper I knew I could make Maxwell nervous." The kick-out? "I decided not to turn away, or jump too high when the keeper went to play the ball so that when it hit me I would be able to try to control it." The loose ball? "When Maxwell kicked it, it smacked me in the stomach and I was able to take off after it right away." The cross-cum-shot? "As I sent it towards the goal, I hit it in such a way that I thought it would go in, but by the time it had reached the middle of the area I knew it was going to hit the post." The goal? "I just saw this orange shirt racing in, I didn't know who it was, but I knew it was going in." The après goal? "I was almost at the cornerflag and I just thought I'm going to stand here for a while and just look at the faces in the crowd as they all jumped about and hugged each other and cheered. It was wonderful."

However, his memories of the celebrations after the match are, not surprisingly, less than clear and he just hopes that the journalists who pressed him for post-match interviews and comments put his rather garbled remarks down to his natural reticence at being interviewed rather than to anything else!

# No 14 Jerren Nixon

Ivan Golac fetched him from Trinidad on a cold December day in 1993, this nimble winger who sometimes seems to float on air. He had been about to return to America when the word came through that Dundee United were interested in his services. The Tayside club may not be amongst the Top Ten best known outfits in the Caribbean, but Nixon needed a break and he feels that he has made a wise choice. Certainly the Tannadice crowd believe he has - they have fallen for him hook, line and sinker. With seven minutes to go in the Cup final he peeled off his outer garments and swapped places with Andy McLaren.....

---

# SEVEN MINUTES OF .. HELL ..

When football is increasingly dominated by tactics and a bland approach, and less and less by individuals, Jerren Nixon is the proverbial breath of fresh air that occasionally blows through the Scottish game. He can dance and shimmy his way along the wing to baffle and deceive the opposition. One thing's for sure, he's got the Tannadice crowd eating out of his hand. "Oh, Nix-on, Oh, Nix-on" the unison cry when he's only warming up. They bow repeatedly when he's playing and the suggestion is that they are not worthy to even lace his boots. And if he scores, he's quite likely to return the compliment with a bow or two of his own.

And Ivan Golac thinks he's magic. To the amusement of many he has told the press that he thinks Nixon is worth not a single penny less than £10 million. Now that's serious money! The player himself realises this might just be an over-inflated valuation, but nonetheless he is flattered by the fact that it certainly focuses attention on him. Whatsmore, such talk serves only to give him confidence.

After all, it's just good clean fun. And fun, it seems, is what Nixon believes football is all about. His happy-go-lucky personality shines through and his smile can warm the darkest day. "I can't get upset if a move breaks down, or I make a mistake, I just have to shrug my shoulders and get on with the game."

And if he has a weakness he'll agree it's his fitness. "I find it hard to last for the full ninety minutes." Back home in Trinidad life was much less frenetic. "You live from one day to the next there. If you don't feel like training then you can go to the beach or to the movies."

It must then have been something of a culture shock to arrive in Scotland. "Training is taken much more seriously here." But Nixon is rapidly acclimatising to the unfamiliar regime. "Slowly my fitness and stamina are improving." And while he misses his family and the Caribbean sunshine he's happy to be playing football in Britain and realises that these are the sacrifices he has to make.

Ostensibly laid-back and gentle, Nixon is also extremely 'streetwise'. "You have to be tough to survive where I come from. I also lived in Brooklyn in New York for a while - so life in Dundee is a bed of roses in comparison!" Here the local kids are forever knocking at his door to ask if he can come out to play and every now and again he might be persuaded to accept and you'll see the boy who is the toast of Tannadice playing kickabout in the street.

In the Cup final he came on in the 83rd minute. Here he describes his feelings as the match progressed.

"I got quite nervous sitting on the bench. You feel so helpless. Mind you, it was a tremendous feeling hearing the crowd chanting your name in that huge stadium every time you came out of the dug-out to warm-up. And when Craig scored I just leapt about and hugged Gary Bollan. All I can remember when I knew I was about to go on was that Paul Hegarty had told us that we should just go out and enjoy every minute of the game. He told us all that it was certainly not beyond the team to beat Rangers. But when I actually went onto the pitch all I kept thinking was that I mustn't do anything wrong. I mustn't be the one who made the mistake which lost United the game! From the minute I started to play I just kept hoping and praying that the final whistle would blow! And when it did I was just so relieved."

"I suppose at the time I didn't fully appreciate what the game meant to everyone. It was a great experience but it was only when we were on our way to the city centre the next day and I looked at the huge crowd in Dundee and saw that everyone was calling our names and reaching out to touch us that I realised what we had done for the people of the city. The fans were just so superb and I was very touched by the way they behaved towards us. It was all very moving."

He presented his winner's medal to the one person that has helped him most throughout his career - his Mum! It now sits proudly in his home in Trinidad.

## No 12 Gary Bollan

He was only thirteen when he signed for Dundee United. He's been a fan ever since and is almost as happy sitting in the crowd at Tannadice as he is out on the pitch. Now that he's the ripe old age of twenty-one, Gary Bollan is something of a veteran campaigner. In 1989 he was a highly acclaimed member of Scotland's Under-16 World Cup squad who, despite losing to the Saudi Arabian side in the final of the competition, did much to restore dwindling faith in the future of the Scottish game. In the Cup final he wore the number 12 shirt, but was never pressed into service and yet, his winner's medal is as valid as those presented to the other players.

---

# THEY ALSO SERVE,
# WHO ONLY SIT AND WAIT

Gary Bollan doesn't look like the nervous type. At just a pinch under six feet tall and weighing in at over twelve stones, you'd think he'd have nerves of steel, but when he found himself on the substitutes' bench in the Cup final he readily admits he succumbed to the odd butterfly or two. There was, he felt, quite a lot of pressure on him. While others in the team were relaxed and full of confidence Bollan was riddled with anxiety.

And yet, for all that, he feels to have been included in the thirteen was not only a tremendous experience, it was a resounding vote of confidence in his ability. The manager clearly thought that, if required, Bollan could make some impact on the game and, although on this occasion, his services were not required the player is philosophical. "Although I was a little disappointed, it was probably all for the best that I wasn't called up," he says, "everyone was playing so well there was no real need to send me on - it might just have broken the momentum."

Such modesty. And while it may be hard to judge, and something of an academic exercise to surmise, just what impact Bollan may have made on the game, nonetheless Ivan Golac didn't choose him just to make up the quorum of players. He was there for a purpose. No-one could say how good he might have been, only how good he is. Bollan clearly has qualities which made him as essential to the team as Guido Van de Kamp or Craig Brewster.

A left-sided player, Bollan has made close on forty appearances for United, sometimes in midfield, more often in defence where only the constancy of Maurice Malpas has prevented him from claiming a regular place in the side. Bollan and Malpas are very different, both in temperament and style. Where Malpas is a general, Bollan is a warrior - immensely powerful and strong. Mind you, power isn't the only aspect of his style of play. His control and distribution stands honest comparison with almost any contemporary, he can work his way out of most tight situations. He has speed and an instinctive sense of timing which make him as effective in attack as he is formidable in defence. And when you watch him charging along the left flank, head down, a determined look on his face, you think - there's a player who might just cause some havoc in the goal area. And he does. There's a man whose shot is bound to be thunderous. And it is.

Bollan has one other speciality: the long throw. With three or four quick strides he arches backwards and delivers the ball with accuracy into the penalty area.

Gary Bollan is more than a player, he is a state of mind. Just the kind of guy you'd want to have on the bench in a Cup final!